Red-Eared Sliders

KATRINA SMITH

Red-Eared Sliders
Project Team
Editor: Thomas Mazorlig
Indexer: Elizabeth Walker
Design Concept: Leah Lococo Ltd.,
Stephanie Krautheim
Design Layout: Angela Stanford

TFH Publications
President/CEO: Glen S. Axelrod
Executive Vice President: Mark E. Johnson
Publisher: Christopher T. Reggio
Production Manager: Kathy Bontz

TFH Publications, Inc.
One TFH Plaza
Third and Union Avenues
Neptune City, NJ 07753

Discovery Communications, LLC. Book Development Team: Marjorie Kaplan, President and General Manager, Animal Planet Media/ Kelly Day, Executive Vice President and General Manager, Discovery Commerce/ Elizabeth Bakacs, Vice President, Licensing and Creative/ JP Stoops, Director, Licensing/ Betsy Ferg, Design Director, Licensing/ Bridget Stoyko, Associate Art Director, Licensing

©2010 Discovery Communications, LLC. Animal Planet and the Animal Planet logo are trademarks of Discovery Communications, LLC, used under license. All rights reserved.animalplanet.com

Printed and bound in China.
09 10 11 12 13   1 3 5 7 9 8 6 4 2

Library of Congress Cataloging-in-Publication Data
Smith, Katrina.
  Red-eared sliders / Katrina Smith.
      p. cm.
  Includes index.
  ISBN 978-0-7938-3709-0 (alk. paper)
  1. Red-eared sliders as pets. 2. Turtles as pets. I. Title.
  SF459.T8S64 2011
  639.3'924–dc22

                        2010041464

This book has been published with the intent to provide accurate and authoritative information in regard to the subject matter within. While every reasonable precaution has been taken in preparation of this book, the author and publisher expressly disclaim responsibility for any errors, omissions, or adverse effects arising from the use or application of the information contained herein. The techniques and suggestions are used at the reader's discretion and are not to be considered a substitute for veterinary care. If you suspect a medical problem consult your veterinarian.

Note: In the interest of concise writing, "he" is used when referring to turtles unless the text is specifically referring to females or males. "She" is used when referring to people. However, the information contained herein is equally applicable to both sexes.

The Leader in Responsible Animal Care for Over 50 Years!®
www.tfh.com

Table of **Contents**

Chapter 1

Why I Adore My

Red-Eared Slider

Red-eared sliders are the most common pet turtle in the world. These mostly aquatic reptiles have been kept as household pets in the United States for more than 70 years. Few turtles are as hardy as the slider. This sturdy nature allows them to be more tolerant of husbandry mistakes than other turtles, although they do need proper care for a long and healthy life. Many keepers are initially attracted to the stunning coloration of juvenile sliders, but it is the slider's ability to adapt and his interactive personality that makes him a common household pet. As hobbyists, herpetoculturists,

The beauty and hardiness of the red-eared slider have made him the most popular pet turtle worldwide.

and scientists have learned more about turtles in the wild and the nutritional and husbandry needs of pet turtles, sliders and other turtles have become more popular than ever.

Keeping a Slider: Brief Overview

Although turtles are not cuddly and they can't be trained like dogs and cats, they can make good pets for the right people. They can learn to identify different members of a household and beg for food in their own way. Although they require a large amount of space for a proper enclosure, they often don't require daily care and can be left alone for long weekends or short business trips. They don't require daily grooming or vaccinations. They don't need live food, and commercially manufactured pelleted foods can make up a large part of the diet.

Because sliders live and eat in the water in large aquariums or ponds, the enclosure will require regular water changes and special filters. This can be difficult to maintain for those with physical limitations or for households with limited space. The average adult slider will need at least a 55- or 75-gallon (208.2- or 283.9-l) aquarium. Be advised that some landlords don't allow aquariums this large. Depending on the type of filtration used, the water may have to be changed once a week or once a month, and water filtration might be a bit noisy as well. Sliders may beg incessantly, causing some people to overfeed them, and they need supplemental heat in the form of basking lights and water heaters. While sliders often don't need to see a veterinarian, if a problem does develop it may be difficult to find a veterinarian who specializes in reptiles. This book will help you decide whether keeping red-eared sliders or other aquatic turtles is for you and will teach you how to care for them.

What Is a Turtle?

Turtles, tortoises, and terrapins are all names given to a reptile whose ribs and backbone are fused together to form a shell. Like other reptiles, a turtle's skin is covered by scales. Instead of having teeth, turtles have a hard bony beak somewhat like a bird's. Although many types of turtles live in the water, they still need to breathe air, and they lay their eggs on land. "Turtle" is usually used to describe a reptile with a shell that lives in or near water most of its life. In England, the term turtle is reserved for sea turtles, and freshwater turtles are called "terrapins," so red-eared sliders are called "red-eared terrapins." In the United States, terrapin used to refer to any turtle commonly used for food, although now the term usually is used to describe one species of turtle, the diamondback terrapin (*Malaclemys terrapin*). "Tortoise" is used for turtles that live exclusively on land. There are more than 300 species or subspecies of turtles.

Red-eared sliders are sometimes referred to as aquatic and sometimes as semi-aquatic. They spend a lot of time in the water and require only a small land section, so for our purposes aquatic is an apt description. We'll use aquatic in this book, but keepers should be aware that both terms get used.

Scientific Names

Scientific names are used by scientists and animal lovers to have a specific name for a specific type of animal. Because people in different areas may have different names for the same species of turtle, a scientific name allows people from many different areas to know they are talking about the same animal. A North American wood turtle might be called a red-legged terrapin in some areas or a wood turtle in others, but if it's called *Glyptemys insculpta*, we can all know what type of turtle we're talking about without confusing it with another species that may have a similar name or description, such as a diamondback terrapin (*Malaclemys terrapin*) or a Central American wood turtle (*Rhinoclemmys pulcherrima*).

A species name is made up of two or three parts. The first part describes the genus, the second part describes the species, and if there's a third part, it describes the subspecies. Closely related species are grouped into a genus (plural: genera) and closely related genera are grouped into a family. So the red-eared slider is *Trachemys scripta elegans*. *Trachemys* is Greek for "rough turtle;" *scripta* is Latin for "written" or "marked" to describe the shell pattern; and *elegans* is Latin for "elegant;" to describe the red mark on each side of the head.

Slider External Anatomy

vertebral scute

foot

carapace

head

costal scute

top view (albino slider)

marginal
scute

claw

vertebral scute

costal scute

marginal
scute

tail

plastron

side view (normal slider)

bridge

Physical Characterisitcs

Sliders and all other turtles have a shell made of bone, and the shell is composed of two or three parts. (There is a famiy of softshelled turtles, but even they have some bones in the shell.) The top shell is the carapace, and the bottom shell is the plastron. An area called the bridge joins the two on each side of the turtle, although some turtles such as box turtles lack a true bridge and have a flexible attachment between the carapace and plastron. Each section of the shell is called a scute. The scutes on the edge of the carapace are called marginals. A thin layer of keratin covers the bone of the shell. Keratin is a protein that makes up feathers in birds and hair in mammals. Some turtles will shed layers of keratin, as a bird will molt and shed feathers, and some turtles do not. Some turtles have a raised ridge along the center of the carapace called a keel.

Sliders are medium-size to large freshwater turtles with an oval shell that has a weak keel and a slightly serrated rear margin. They have webbed feet, and the hind feet are wide to allow for swimming in deep water. They are called "sliders" because of their love of basking in the sun on exposed logs and rocks. When threatened or approached by a potential predator, they'll "slide"

back into the water, and quite quickly at that.

Although baby red-eared sliders are tiny, roughly the size of a quarter when first hatched and barely weighing 5 to 10 grams, some full-grown adult females can reach 11 inches (28 cm) in length and weigh over five pounds (2.3 kg). Males reach sexual maturity at a shell size between roughly 3.5 and 4.5 inches (8.9 and 11.4 cm), and females between 6.5 and 7.5 inches (16.5 and 19 cm). Males have elongated, slightly curved front claws, and a longer, thicker tail than females. Males use their long front claws in a courtship display in which they gently brush or "flutter" their nails against the female's head to get her attention. Although turtles don't have external ears as people do, they do have ear canals and inner ear bones. Their tympanum, or ear drum, is on the outside of the head. Research shows that

Red-eared sliders have webbed feet and strong legs, making them powerful swimmers.

turtles can likely hear low frequencies very well, and probably hear best in the region of 200 to 700 Hz.

Coloration

Hatchlings of all slider species and subspecies start out with a bright green carapace with yellow markings on each section or scute, and a yellow plastron with dark spots or circles on some or all of the scutes. The skin is green to olive brown, with yellow stripes on the head and legs. As the turtle ages, the colors turn darker, and eventually the carapace becomes olive brown, black, or blackish gray, with muted yellow lines on the carapace. The dark spots on the plastron will turn black and might take up more of the shell than when the turtle was young. In very old turtles, especially males, the entire turtle may become completely black, or a mottled black and gray. These dark-colored turtles are referred to as melantistic.

Growth Rings

As a turtle ages, the shell adds a growth ring to each scute. Some people believe, incorrectly, that you can tell a turtle's age by counting the rings. While some wild turtles in climates with a noticeable winter and summer temperature contrast may put down only one ring a year, some turtles may add more than one ring in a good year when food is plentiful or may not add any rings during a lean year, such as during a prolonged drought. As the turtle ages and adds more rings, the rings will start to run together at the edges, so that it's

impossible to tell one ring from another after about 20 rings develop. To further complicate matters, older turtles often rub their shells smooth, especially if there is sand or other rough substrates in the environment.

Middle-aged sliders may have *rugosa*, which are wavy ridges that build up on the sides of the shell, running across the length of the carapace. Some truly elderly turtles might have completely smooth shells, so that no rings or even growth lines are visible on the shell.

Sliders in the Wild

Wild sliders live in freshwater habitats of almost any variety, but they prefer quiet waters with soft bottoms, an abundance of aquatic plants, and suitable basking sites. They may have extensive home ranges that can include several bodies of water that they frequently travel between on overland trips. They can be found in or near salt marshes, ponds, lakes, and rivers of the United States, Mexico, and Central and South America. In the wild, the northern populations will hibernate in the winter. Even turtles found in southern regions of the United States may hibernate for short periods.

The Red-Eared Slider Family Tree

Sliders are part of the turtle family Emydidae, which is the largest family of living turtles. Common pet aquatic turtles in the family Emydidae include sliders (genus *Trachemys*), painted turtles (*Chrysemys picta*), map turtles (genus *Graptemys*), red-bellies and cooters (genus *Pseudemys*), the

Males versus Females

It is easy to tell the difference between adult males and females, but almost impossible to tell in hatchling or juvenile sliders. Adult males have much longer front nails and longer, thicker tails—note the claws on the male albino slider in the photo above. Males tend to stay smaller than females, and even the largest adult males may be two to four inches (5 to 10.2 cm) smaller than the largest females. Unfortunately, sexual dimorphism—the ability to tell males and females apart by appearance—isn't apparent until sliders reach roughly four inches (10.2 cm) in top shell length. Before reaching that size, all sliders look like females, with short nails and short tails.

If space is a consideration, it's better to get a male, since male aquatic turtles stay smaller than females. Additionally, females may lay eggs, even if they've never been with a male. If there's no egg-laying area, they may become egg-bound--the eggs become stuck inside the female (see Chapter 4 for more information on egg binding). Egg binding is a serious condition that needs veterinary attention. While all sliders become darker with age and lose their bright hatchling colors, males tend to become melanistic, turning almost completely black and/or gray as they age.

diamondback terrapin (*Malaclemys terrapin*), and chicken turtles (*Deirochelys reticularia*).

Slider Species and Subspecies

There are two species of sliders in the United States, *Trachemys gaigeae*, the Big Bend slider of Texas which appears infrequently in the pet trade, and *Trachemys scripta*, which consists of three subspecies in the United States; there are other subspecies that range as far south as northern South America. The red-eared slider (*T. scripta elegans*) is the most commonly kept of the three, followed by the yellow-bellied slider (*T. scripta scripta*), and the Cumberland slider (*T. scripta troosti*). All three subspecies grow to about the same adult size, typically 6 to 8 inches (15.2 to 20.3 cm) for males,

and 8 to 10 inches (20.3 to 25.4 cm) for females, although some larger and smaller specimens may be found. There are other species of sliders native to Mexico, Central America, South America, and the Caribbean, such as the Belize slider (*Trachemys venusta*), that are captive bred for the pet trade, but these turtles get even larger than United States sliders and do not hibernate.

Red-Eared Slider

Red-eared sliders are the most common subspecies of slider in the pet trade. They are known for the distinguishing red stripe or blotch behind each eye. Some may have a red spot or thin red line on the center of the head. They have yellow stripes on their heads and legs, along with narrow chin stripes and a pattern of at least one black spot on each scute on the plastron. Occasionally a color variation of the red-eared slider, called the Rio Grande slider, is seen in the pet trade, but this is just a variation of *T. s. elegans*, and not a separate subspecies. Rio Grande sliders may have a more pointed, upturned snout, more red coloration on the head, and a more heavily patterned carapace. Other color patterns or "morphs" have been captive bred by hobbyists and herpetoculturists (professional reptile breeders), and these include albino, caramel, clown, and pastel color variations.

Yellow-Bellied Slider

The yellow-bellied slider (*Trachemys scripta scripta*) looks very similar to the red-eared slider but has a wide yellow stripe or check mark behind each eye instead of the red blotch. The broad stripe often continues as a lone thin stripe along the neck. Yellow-bellied sliders have fewer spots on the plastron than red-ears—usually there are only two or four spots on the plastron closer to the head of a yellow-belly. There is usually a yellow stripe forming an arrow over the nose of a yellow-bellied slider as well, and they may have a higher-domed carapace when fully grown.

Cumberland Slider

The Cumberland slider (*Trachemys scripta troosti*) has a broad yellow or orange stripe on the side of the head instead of a distinct red blotch, although there might be a patch of red inside the stripe. The chin stripes will be much broader too. Cumberland sliders often have stripes on their legs that form whorls or bull's-eye patterns. The shell of a Cumberland may have more whorls and patterns than that of a red-eared or yellow-bellied slider.

Natural Range

Red-ears occupy the Mississippi River system from Illinois and Ohio to the Gulf of Mexico west to Texas. Yellow-bellies range from southern Virginia to northern Florida. Cumberlands are found in the upper portions of the Cumberland and Tennessee rivers, from southwestern Virginia and Kentucky to northeastern Alabama. Where the range of the subspecies meet,

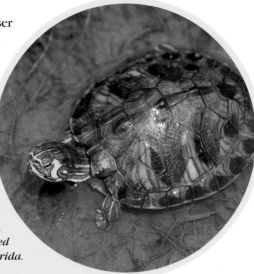

The yellow-bellied slider has a wide yellow mark behind the eyes. This young turtle was photographed in northern Florida.

Cumberland sliders have smaller markings behind the eyes than yellow-bellies do.

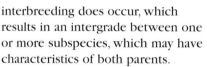

interbreeding does occur, which results in an intergrade between one or more subspecies, which may have characteristics of both parents.

Unfortunately, escaped or unwanted pet sliders have been released over much of the world. Because of their hardy nature, there are "feral" or invasive populations living where they shouldn't be. The result is that they can be found in almost any state in the United States, and in many Asian and European countries. Keep in mind that just because you find a wild red-eared slider living in your area doesn't necessarily mean it is a turtle found naturally in that area. Because red-eared sliders in particular have been released as unwanted pets in non-native areas, they may be out-competing native species and interbreeding with native populations of yellow-bellied and

Cumberland sliders, which threatens the ecological integrity of the native turtles.

Slider History

Hatchling red-eared sliders used to be sold as almost disposable children's pets in dime stores and department stores. Tiny green turtles were sold with a shallow plastic pool and a miniature plastic palm tree. Some had their shells painted with bright designs. They were so popular that turtle farms sprang up in the southern United States, mostly in Louisiana. Dozens of turtle farms produced millions of eggs. Sadly, most of those "dime store turtles" died within a few months of purchase, as the tiny containers did not allow for proper filtration and thermoregulation, the paint affected the turtles' health, and information on husbandry and food requirements was hard to find.

In 1975, the sale of hatchling turtles as pets in connection with a business was banned in the United States by a Food and Drug Administration regulation when it became evident that thousands of children were contracting salmonellosis from their pet turtles. While all reptiles have the potential to carry the salmonella organism, hatchling sliders were more likely than any other reptile to be purchased as inexpensive children's pets, making them a greater disease risk. Turtle farms continue to breed and hatch out millions of sliders, but most hatchlings are exported for pet sales overseas. Larger turtles may be sold as pets or exported to overseas food markets, and some are used for scientific studies or comparative anatomy classes.

Where to Get a Slider

There are several options for acquiring a pet turtle. Pet stores, large-scale dealers, breeders, and hobbyists sell them. Animal shelters, reptile rescues, turtle and tortoise societies, humane societies, and other animal rescues often have them for adoption, and private keepers may offer them for adoption. Some breeders and dealers will sell their turtles online and have them shipped to your home with next-day service. Some rescues will also ship turtles. Turtles should never be shipped through the United States Postal Service, though, because that is illegal.

Sliders in pet stores are often from large turtle farms in the southern United States and have probably lived in large outdoor ponds before going to the pet store, so they may still think and act like wild turtles when first brought home. However, since sliders are so adaptable, they quickly learn to adjust to family living. A slider with a four-inch-long (10.2-cm) shell purchased from a pet store is probably about three to five years old.

A turtle from a shelter or rescue may or may not come with a history, and the exact age may or may not be known. If it was surrendered by a family that acquired it as a hatchling, you'll likely know how old your turtle is, and he may or may not have veterinary records. He will probably be very personable, as he is already used to people.

A professional breeder or hobbyist will likely know how old the turtle is and from where the parent stock originated, since he hatched out the eggs and likely keeps records. A large turtle farm, wholesaler, or large-scale dealer will not keep such records, as they have such a large number of turtles that they can't keep track of individual animals.

Lifespan and Aging

Although aquatic turtles don't have the long lifespans that box turtles and tortoises do, they can be long lived. In the wild, adults can reach 20 to 30 years old. Pet turtles have the ability to live much longer with proper care. One red-eared slider in Maryland lived to be 67 years old, and 30-year-old pet sliders are more common than you'd think.

Adorable hatchling sliders are available frequently, but they are less hardy than adults and older juveniles.

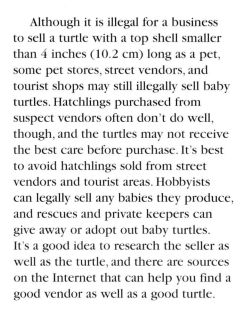

Although it is illegal for a business to sell a turtle with a top shell smaller than 4 inches (10.2 cm) long as a pet, some pet stores, street vendors, and tourist shops may still illegally sell baby turtles. Hatchlings purchased from suspect vendors often don't do well, though, and the turtles may not receive the best care before purchase. It's best to avoid hatchlings sold from street vendors and tourist areas. Hobbyists can legally sell any babies they produce, and rescues and private keepers can give away or adopt out baby turtles. It's a good idea to research the seller as well as the turtle, and there are sources on the Internet that can help you find a good vendor as well as a good turtle.

Wild Collection

Depending on where you live, it may or may not be legal to take a turtle from the wild. There are also ethical considerations for taking a wild animal from its native habitat, as well as ecological ones. Collection for the pet trade has decimated some populations of turtles, and many species are in danger because of overcollection as well as habitat loss.

A wild turtle, particularly an adult, will be less likely to acclimate to a captive environment and might be so stressed that he refuses to eat and eventually passes away. Removing an adult turtle from a wild population has enormous ecological drawbacks, as turtles survive as a group by producing a few eggs each for many, many years—the longer the turtle lives, the more eggs it can produce, and the older females have been shown to lay more eggs each year than younger females. Most eggs and hatchlings in the wild are eaten by predators, so removing a hatchling or juvenile will have less environmental impact on the wild population, and a juvenile will be more likely to acclimate to being kept as a pet. Since sliders have been released in large numbers in areas where they are not native, it may be possible to find a wild, feral slider in your area where they are not native. If this is the case, it's usually legal to keep him as a pet.

Turtles and the Law

It's important to research the local and state regulations to make sure it's legal to keep a pet turtle in your area. Many states, counties, and cities have regulations regarding the possession of wildlife or exotic pets, and sliders are often considered one or the other. Exotics are considered to be any nondomesticated animal not native to a state or country. Although sliders have been bred in captivity and kept as pets for decades, they're usually not considered domesticated in many regulations. In Detroit, Michigan, for example, it's illegal to keep any reptile, including turtles. Oregon completely bans the keeping of red-eared sliders; they're considered invasive exotics. In Florida, it's illegal to sell or breed pet red-eared sliders unless one has a special permit, and the red-eared sliders cannot be sold in the state unless they are color morphs, such as albinos. New Jersey requires a permit to keep turtles, and Delaware requires a permit for exotic animals. The United Kingdom and other European countries ban the importation of red-

eared sliders. Maryland requires a permit for the possession of turtles less than four inches (10.2 cm) in carapace length.

Check with your local state wildlife agency and animal control, and review county or city ordinances to see whether a pet turtle is legal in your area. The phone numbers for these agencies can be found online or in the blue pages of most phone books.

No matter how you acquire your slider, it's always a good idea to get a receipt, adoption contract, or some sort of written proof of when and

Being a Turtle Advocate

Please report the sale of hatchling red-eared sliders to the proper authorities; there is a federal regulation that prevents the sale of turtles under 4 inches (10.2 cm) in length. Doing so can help save the lives of turtles and prevent uniformed owners from buying a cute little hatchling without understanding his needs or his potential size. The regional Food and Drug Administration (FDA) office can be found in the blue pages of a phone book and online, and the FDA will accept consumer complaints about the sale of hatchling sliders.

Closely inspect any turtle before purchasing him. A healthy slider has clear eyes and no bumps, lumps, or wounds on his head and neck.

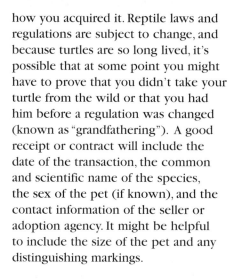

how you acquired it. Reptile laws and regulations are subject to change, and because turtles are so long lived, it's possible that at some point you might have to prove that you didn't take your turtle from the wild or that you had him before a regulation was changed (known as "grandfathering"). A good receipt or contract will include the date of the transaction, the common and scientific name of the species, the sex of the pet (if known), and the contact information of the seller or adoption agency. It might be helpful to include the size of the pet and any distinguishing markings.

Should You Start with a Hatchling?

Although baby turtles are small and incredibly cute, they eventually grow up and get larger, and their bright coloration will darken as they get older. While a baby turtle might need only a 10-gallon (38-l) aquarium at first, it will still end up needing a larger aquarium later on, and females need more room than males. Most turtles will acclimate to a household with the proper care, so age usually isn't an issue with "bonding"—an older turtle can learn the household routine as well as a baby can; it will just take a bit longer. Plus, hatchlings can be fragile at first, and many die in their first year. It's impossible to tell whether a hatchling is a male or female, so if future enclosure size is an issue, it's best to acquire an older turtle that's obviously a male rather than risk starting with a hatchling of unknown sex. Although some breeders and turtle farms incubate the eggs at certain temperatures in an attempt to obtain only one sex in one set of eggs, it's still impossible to say with 100 percent certainty whether a hatchling will be a male or female. If size isn't an issue, then go with your heart's content.

Picking a Healthy Slider

A healthy slider will be active and inquisitive, with a rather smooth hard shell and bright eyes. He should try to get away when held at first. In a pet store, some may be basking on a platform or log, but when approached they should look alert and be ready to jump back into the water. If a slider doesn't move on the basking spot

FAMILY-FRIENDLY TIP

A Good Child's Pet?

While turtles have the reputation of being children's pets, this does not necessarily make them the ideal child's pet. Some turtles may tolerate handling, but most dislike being held. Turtles can bite, and large adults can pack a hard bite that may break the skin. They also have sharp nails on their hand feet and, as with all other reptiles, have the potential to carry salmonella. Adults should always be the primary care givers, and anyone handling a turtle or caring for it should always immediately wash his or her hands afterward.

when you walk up to the cage, it may be sick, especially if it's sleeping with its head down on the basking platform. In the water, some may be investigating the enclosure while others swim to the front of the cage to see whether you have food. Although sliders will sleep underwater, they should wake up when they hear or feel activity in the water or outside the enclosure.

Physical Inspection

Look for any abscesses, injuries, or scrapes on the nose, eyes, feet, head, neck, and tail. Other turtles may nip off the tip of another turtle's tail, toes, or nose, or bite the back of the neck of another turtle in aggression. A deep wound will need veterinary attention, as will a swollen toe or foot. If a toe or tail tip is missing, but the injury is completely healed with no open wound, the turtle will be fine. Look to see whether there are any lumps or bumps on the head. A lump on the side of the head is likely an ear infection that will need a trip to the veterinarian.

Watch the turtle basking for a few minutes or hold it for a minute to make sure there are no bubbles or discharge from the nose or mouth, which could indicate a respiratory infection. If you can get the turtle to open its mouth, you should see pink tissue. If there is a white build-up or heavy strings of saliva, the turtle may have an infection. If the eyelids are puffy or the eyes won't open, he could have an eye or respiratory infection.

Hold the turtle. Does he feel heavy for his size or does he feel as if there's nothing but shell there? A healthy turtle should feel heavy, almost like a stone or brick of the same size. An extremely underweight turtle may also float and have trouble diving under the water. The turtle should squirm or try to get away when you hold him, or try to pull into its shell to hide; a hatchling or wild turtle is more likely to pull into the shell while a captive-bred adult or older juvenile is more likely to try to escape. Gently tug on a hind foot. A healthy turtle will be able to respond quickly by pulling the leg back with some force. If the turtle responds weakly or is indifferent to being touched, he may be sick. A healthy turtle may hiss when first handled, which is a quick exhale of breath as the turtle quickly pulls his head in. This is different from the raspy breathing of a turtle with a serious respiratory infection.

Feel the shell and look for any discolored spots that don't match the rest of the shell. Pay close attention to the marginal scutes. Is there a discoloration along the outer edges? A shell infection called shell rot can look like dark pits on the shell, or appear as lighter or darker areas that don't quite match the surrounding shell. Shell rot may cause soft areas, so gently press on the entire shell to make sure all of it is solid. Shell rot may also smell bad, so don't be afraid to get your nose close to any suspect areas on the shell—just make sure the turtle doesn't bite your nose!

Inspecting the Surroundings

If you're picking your turtle from a group in a pet store or at a dealer's table, check to see how crowded the enclosure is. Too many turtles in one enclosure can cause stress, which may cause health issues even weeks after purchase, as well as lead to bites and claw marks from other turtles. Crowded conditions can lead to dirty water, which can also cause health problems.

A pet store should provide their aquatic turtles with a basking spot and a heat light and shouldn't mix turtles of drastically different sizes or with species of turtles from other countries. You want your slider to be kept only with other sliders or at least only US species, such as painted or map turtles, to minimize disease transmission between turtles from other parts of the world. If you see red-eared sliders being kept in the same enclosure with African, Asian, or South American species, or other animals such as lizards, snakes, or tortoises, you might want to look elsewhere for your pet.

Do You Need a Pair?

While aquatic turtles prefer to bask in groups, they also need a great deal of space, and few families are willing to provide the extra space needed to keep two sliders together. Overcrowding can lead to stress and fighting between two turtles, possibly causing injuries or death. Unless you are willing to provide a very large habitat with extra hide spots—a fenced-in backyard pond, for example—it's probably best to keep just one slider per enclosure.

If You Can't Keep Your Slider

When you decide to get a red-eared slider or other aquatic turtle, you should plan on keeping and caring for your pet for his entire life span—at least 20 years. Despite your best intentions, a lot can change in two decades. Some potential changes could make it impossible for you to keep your turtle. If for some reason you can no longer care for your slider, you might want to consider some of these options.

Check with family and friends to see if they might want a turtle. Make sure the interested person understands what's required to keep a turtle properly before you actually give your slider to her.

Some herpetological societies and turtle and tortoise societies have adoption programs that take in pet reptiles. However, people surrender red-eared sliders to these organizations all the time, so they may not have room for your turtle. It doesn't hurt to check, but don't be overly hopeful of success.

Some pet stores, veterinary offices, grocery stores, and other local businesses allow people to post pet adoption ads. Put together a flyer and post it in several of these in your area. You also can place an ad at www.petfinder.com or www.craigslist.org.

When trying to find a home for your slider through one of these methods, screen potential adopters carefully. You want to be sure the adopter provides the same quality of care that you do.

Contact your local animal control agency or humane society to see if they will accept turtles. Although you might be tempted to contact a nature center or zoo, most of them already have all the animals they can care for, and they probably get calls every week from people trying to place sliders. Some pet stores may take sliders, but you have to decide if you want your turtle to be sold to someone else.

Releasing a slider to a pond or lake is not an alternative. This is illegal in most states for several reasons. Red-eared sliders are not native to much of the United States. They can cause environmental issues for our native turtles. There is also the risk of a slider transmitting a disease to our native wildlife.

Chapter 2

What a Slider
Needs

Many people prefer to keep their slider indoors so they can interact with him. Others find it easier to maintain a backyard pond and allow their slider to hibernate over the winter. Either way will be fine so long as the turtle has everything he needs. There is no real single "right way" for keeping turtles, although some are better, or easier, than others. Don't be afraid to experiment or think outside the box, so long as your setup meets all of your turtle's needs. Your imagination is the limit when it comes to housing a turtle.

Red-eared sliders and other aquatic turtles all need the same basic housing supplies. The main requirement is a large water area, such as an aquarium, indoor pond, or outdoor pond in an escape-proof area. They also need a basking area or haul-out spot and water filtration. If kept indoors, they'll also need a heat light and a siphon for changing the water. A water heater may or may not be necessary depending on the temperatures in the home. Ultraviolet light is highly recommended, as are hiding spots.

Types of Enclosures

Aquariums

Glass or acrylic aquariums are the most commonly used containers for keeping turtles indoors. These aquariums can be quite attractive, but they can be heavy and expensive. For keepers who aren't handy, premade stands are available for most aquariums. Premade screens are sold in sizes to match the aquariums. If getting an aquarium, avoid tanks sold as terrariums, which are usually made of lighter-weight materials and are not designed to hold large volumes of water. Such a terrarium might be acceptable for a small semi-aquatic turtle such as a stinkpot, or common musk turtle, but not for a slider.

Stock Tanks

Stock tanks are water troughs traditionally used with cattle and other livestock. They are relatively inexpensive, extremely durable, and come in several sizes, from 35 to 700 gallons (132.5 to 2649.8 l). You can purchase a stock tank at farm supply stores, some home improvement and plant stores, and some specialty pet stores. Stock tanks are a fraction of the price of a similarly sized aquarium. They are not as attractive as aquariums, and premade stands aren't available for them, so you will have to make your own. Some keepers use old coffee tables or dressers as stands for the smaller stock tanks. You can also put stock tanks on top of cinder blocks. A tablecloth or homemade skirt can be used to fit over a home-made stand for aesthetics, and the outside of the stock tank can be framed or decorated to match a room's décor.

There are two basic varieties of stock tanks, galvanized metal and plastic. Galvanized metal tanks need

Tank Size

When considering an enclosure for an aquatic turtle, a good rule of thumb is roughly ten gallons per inch (38 l per 2.5 cm) of shell measured from the front to the back of the carapace. So a 6-inch (15.2-cm) slider would need at minimum a 55-gallon (208.2-l) aquarium or indoor pond, although larger is usually better. Two adult females should have at least a 125-gallon (473.2-l) enclosure.

You can house your slider in a large glass aquarium. Furnish the habitat with filter, basking platform, thermometer, and lights as shown here.

to be lined with a pond liner to prevent potentially dangerous metals from leaching into the water and to extend the life of the tank. Plastic stock tanks—typically sold in a dark gray color—are very lightweight for their size and do not need an additional liner. Some stock tanks are sold with pre-installed drains and plugs, so that a working spigot and hose can be attached for quick and easy draining without the use of a pump or siphon.

If keeping your turtles outside in the summer, a locking screened lid can be built and drilled directly onto the lip of a stock tank to keep out predators or to keep indoor pets from getting into the tank. Some people even place a stock tank on a homemade frame with wheels, so that the stock tank can be brought indoors in the winter and wheeled outside in the summer. If using a stock tank outside, keep in mind that an above-ground enclosure may heat up faster than a pond in the ground, so watch your water temperatures to make sure the turtle doesn't overheat.

Storage Bins

Plastic storage bins—sometimes called storage totes—can be used for smaller turtles, as short-term housing, or as hospital tanks. They are inexpensive but not as hardy as stock tanks. Also, they can't hold large volumes of water—the sides may bow out when they're too full. A handy person can prevent this by making a frame to support a storage bin. Water heaters will melt a plastic storage bin, so if using a water heater with a bin, make sure the heater does not come in contact with the plastic.

Some keepers use stock tanks for housing sliders and other aquatic turtles. These weigh and cost less than similarly sized aquariums.

Ponds

A homemade custom-built indoor pond can be a simple utilitarian wooden frame with a pond liner, or it can be designed to be a focal point in a living room, indoor patio, or finished basement with wooden paneling, potted plants, and other decorations. Outdoor ponds can be attractive centerpieces to a yard, but either the yard or the pond itself must be escape-proof to prevent the turtle from leaving the yard. Outdoor ponds can also be higher maintenance than some people prefer. Some municipalities have regulations against backyard ponds or require the property owner to obtain a permit before starting a pond.

Although ponds are among the best options for housing sliders and other large turtles, few households are able to accommodate a pond. For this reason, pond construction and maintenance are discussed only briefly. Those wishing to learn more about ponds are encouraged to obtain books or magazines that specialize in ponds and research Internet sources.

Enclosure Size

Start with the largest enclosure you can afford. A hatchling turtle can start out in a 10- or 20-gallon (38- or 75.7-l) enclosure but will outgrow it within a year or so. A 55-gallon (208.2-l) tank might seem huge for a hatchling, but you can start with a lower water level and increase it as the turtle grows. An adult slider will need at least a 55-gallon tank (208.2-l), although most females and many adult males will end up needing 75 gallons (284 l) or more for one turtle.

Determining Aquarium and Pond Sizes

Many keepers have a hard time determining the capacity of the aquarium or pond they have. If you already have a roughly rectangular tank or pond, but aren't sure what volume of water it holds, try this calculation, but keep in mind that you might have to round to the nearest tank size: Length x Width x Height)/ 231

For example, if the exterior of my aquarium is 36 inches long, 18 inches wide, and 16 inches tall:

36 x 18 x 16 = 10368.

10368 divided by 231 = 44.9 gallons, so I have a 40-gallon tank. I measured the outside of my tank, not the inside, which is why the volume is larger than the advertised size of a 40-gallon aquarium.

If you have a pond and you are considering adding a turtle but aren't sure of the gallons, try this calculation for feet instead of inches:

Average Length x Average Width x Average Depth x 7.48 = Pond Gallons

So a pond that is about 8 feet long, 2 feet deep, and 3 feet wide (which really isn't a very large pond), will be about 359 gallons, which is just large enough for one or two sliders to live in year-round, if the pond is in a relatively warm climate.

Remember that not all aquariums of the same volume are the same dimensions. For example, 20-gallon (75.7-l) aquariums often come in "tall" or "long" sizes. A 20-gallon tall is 17 inches tall x 13 inches wide x 24 inches long (43.2 x 33 x 61 cm). A 20-gallon long is 13 inches tall x 13 inches wide x 30 inches long (33 x 33 x 76.2 cm). "Breeder" tanks are wider and shorter than regular aquariums. For example, a 50-gallon (189.3-l) breeder is shorter but wider than a traditional 55-gallon (208.2-l) tank. While long or breeder tanks are preferable for turtles, because their length and width give them more square feet to move about, their area alone is not as critical as having enough space overall for exercise, thermoregulation, and proper filtration. Some species of turtles, such as muds, musks, and softshells, do better with long and breeder tanks, but the extra area those tanks provide is not as critical with sliders, although

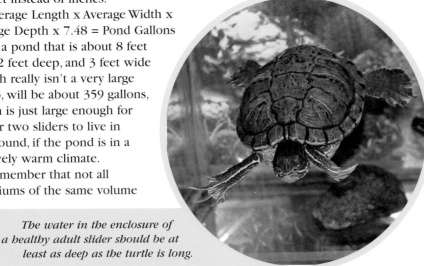

The water in the enclosure of a healthy adult slider should be at least as deep as the turtle is long.

long and breeder-style tanks are ideal for hatchlings and juveniles.

Indoor Enclosures

Although some keepers will argue that an outdoor pond is the most natural way to house a turtle, an indoor enclosure can provide interaction between you and your pet and a measure of security that is difficult to duplicate with outdoor enclosures. It's often easier to monitor the health of an indoor turtle, too, and not all climates are suitable for housing sliders outdoors.

Placing an Indoor Enclosure

An indoor enclosure needs to be close enough to a sink, window, or door to allow for draining the enclosure and refilling with water. Some siphons come in 50-foot (15.2-m) lengths, and water hoses can be longer. Take year-round weather conditions into consideration. It may seem fine to fill a tank with a water hose from an outdoor faucet through the window in the summer, but will this work in the winter?

Aquariums and ponds are heavy. Make sure that the floor and any stands will support the weight of the tank or pond. A coffee table or dresser can double as an inexpensive aquarium or pond stand, but make sure it can hold the weight of a tank full of water. Water weighs approximately 8.4 pounds (3.8 kg) per gallon (3.8 l), so a 55-gallon (208.2-l) tank filled to the top would weigh about 459 pounds (208.2 kg). Also keep in mind that children might be curious about an aquarium. Is the

A 20-gallon (75.7-l) tank set up for hatchling sliders. The basking spot is a piece of cork bark, which the turtles can climb easily.

Basking spot in an indoor pond. The rubber mat provides traction so the turtle can climb up and bask.

29

tank tall enough that children can't put their hands into it? Is the stand sturdy enough that children can't pull or knock over the aquarium? Some metal stands may have to be bolted to the floor or wall if there are toddlers in the area.

Be prepared in the advent of a leak and for accidental drips when cleaning the tank and filter. Will a leaking tank or filter damage the flooring or carpeting? Will a landlord allow you to keep a large tank?

Do not place a tank in direct sunlight, as this can cause the tank to overheat. Contrary to common belief, beneficial UVB light from the sun cannot pass through regular glass, so placing an aquarium next to a window will not give the turtle access to UVB light (see section on UVB lights for more on this topic).

Basking Spot

A basking spot or haul-out spot is needed for your turtle to climb out of the water and warm himself under a heat light or the sun. Basking is a way for turtles to raise their core body temperature for proper digestion, metabolism, and immune function, as well as for shell health. For typical aquarium setups, the water takes up about 2/3 to ¾ of the available space in the tank, so keep this in mind when looking for a basking spot.

Although other sources may recommend using gravel to create a slope for basking or to use rocks as a basking area, those items have drawbacks. Gravel takes up valuable water space and doesn't allow much of a water level if it's used as the sole source for a basking spot. Rocks can also take up a large area, and they can have sharp edges that can scrape a shell, which can lead to shell infections. Rocks can also fall and injure a turtle, trap a turtle underwater, or crack a glass tank. If rocks are used as a naturalistic basking spot, consider using nontoxic epoxy or aquarium sealant to bond the rocks together so that they can't be dislodged.

Buying a Basking Platform

When it comes to buying or making a basking spot, you're limited by your imagination only. Pet stores and online catalogs sell various ceramic or plastic ramps, as well as floating basking spots that affix to the side of the aquarium and move with the water level. However, store-bought platforms rarely come in sizes large enough to accommodate a full-grown slider, particularly a large female. Some keepers have reported that their turtles eat the hard foam platforms, too. For hatchlings and juveniles, though, they can be quite handy.

Floating cork bark can be found in some specialty pet stores and at reptile shows. This is great for smaller turtles, but it needs something to keep it positioned under the heat light. A hole can be drilled into one or more corners, and the cork bark attached to a frame to keep it in place or reinforce it as a basking spot for larger turtles. A new piece of cork bark may turn the water dark for the first few weeks

Small Tanks Don't Make Small Turtles

There is a common belief that turtles and other reptiles grow only to the size of their cage. This is just a myth. A small tank will not result in a small adult turtle. A healthy, well-cared for slider will grow to be the appropriate adult size no matter how small or large the enclosure. If a juvenile turtle isn't growing, it might be time to review husbandry techniques or visit a veterinarian to see whether there's an underlying problem.

that it's used, but this isn't a cause for concern and will decrease with time and water changes. Very rarely, a slider will decide he wants to pick apart floating cork bark for entertainment. If a turtle is eating or constantly biting off pieces of a basking area or artificial plants, remove them immediately and offer a replacement of some sort.

Making a Basking Platform

Home-made basking platforms can be inexpensive or elaborate, and sometimes both. Plastic egg crate screen or louver, sold as a light diffuser in home improvement stores, is a simple, inexpensive way to make basking platforms of any size to fit any aquarium or turtle. The plastic can be cut to create three, four, or five pieces, depending on what it's intended to do. A heavy file or an electric drill or Dremel-type rotary tool equipped with a grinding mechanism is needed to file down any sharp edges left over when the pieces are cut or broken to create the desired sizes. The most basic frame has three pieces, attached to form an inverted "U". The middle cross piece is attached to the two side pieces with electrical zip ties or fishing line at an angle that allows the bottom of the cross piece to rest in the water. If water levels are going to fluctuate, then a fourth or fifth piece can be added to the ends of the cross piece and loosely attached with zip ties, so that the ends float with the water level. The author prefers electrical zip ties to fishing line, but some feel that it's easier to start over with fishing line if the finished product

isn't up to snuff or if a piece breaks later during use.

For large turtles or for very large aquariums or ponds, you can make a basking frame from PVC pipe. The pipe pieces will form a rectangular frame with additional pieces used as legs. You can attach egg crate, cork bark, or other materials to form a sloping platform, enabling the turtle to climb easily onto it. If you want something more natural looking, a large piece or two of cork bark can be screwed straight onto a PVC frame or attached with electrical zip ties after you drill holes into the back and the pipes. To hold the platform in place when using it with large or heavy turtles, you can fill the legs with concrete or gravel or attach a crosspiece on the bottom that is weighed down with rocks or a cinder block.

One of the author's homemade basking platforms. The frame and supports are PVC pipes and the platform is plastic egg crate.

You can use natural pieces of driftwood, tree branches, or stumps provided that they can be positioned safely. The turtle should be able to easily climb completely out of the water and not be accidentally stuck under a heavy branch. It's a good idea to scrub pieces of natural wood and rock with a stiff brush and heavily rinse them with plain water before putting them into the enclosure. This will help remove any unwanted dirt or hidden insects from natural cage decorations. If bricks or cement are being used for any part of the tank, soak them in a bucket of water over night to help rinse off any potential chemicals that might be on the material.

Some Concerns

Make sure that the basking platform doesn't double as an escape route for the turtle. A screen or lid of some kind might be needed to keep the turtle from using the basking platform as a ladder to reach the top of the tank. A screen doesn't have to cover the entire tank, just the basking area, if that's what you prefer. Some keepers have a piece of sheet metal custom cut to fit onto the lip of the tank with holes cut out to allow for a heat light and UVB light. This can help hold in heat and keep the turtles from climbing out, and it helps to decrease evaporation. If you don't have the tools for this, a home improvement store or a handy friend may be able to cut the metal for you or at least recommend someone who can.

Above-Tank Basking Platform

One way to increase water space and make your aquarium useful for a longer time is to build or purchase an above-tank basking platform (ATBP). This is essentially an enclosure over one end of the tank with a ramp leading up to it. The enclosure will allow the tank to be completely filled with water, while still giving the turtle a basking area and preventing his escape from the tank.

The ATBP could be in the middle of the tank, where it would need two sides, or at the end of the tank, where it will need three sides. If using a wooden frame, paint or epoxy all

Water Depth

Red-eared sliders are often found in ponds and lakes in the wild, so they are adapted to handle deeper water. Don't be afraid of making the water too deep, so long as there's an easily accessible basking spot. For a healthy turtle, the water should be at least as deep as the shell is long, although it can be much deeper. If you're worried about the water being too deep, add an extra underwater resting or climbing spot, such as a piece of decorative wood, or add a bit of plastic lattice work or egg crate screen to the back wall of the enclosure. If you've recently rescued a slider that's not used to deep water or brought home a small hatchling, you can start with shallow water for the first few days and gradually add more volume over the next few days.

Sliders need a basking spot that reaches 85° to 90°F (29.4° to 32.2°C). Keep the lights on for 13 to 14 hours each day.

surfaces so that they will resist molding and warping. The basking area can be made from wood, egg crate screen, Plexiglas, or other sturdy material. A ramp leading up to the basking area can be made from similar materials, but avoid wood for the ramp, as it will be partially submerged. Some keepers even use floating "turtle docks" to form the ramp. The sides of the ATBP can be constructed with a combination of wood, Plexiglas, PVC pipe, and/ or plastic-coated wire, depending on what's available and your comfort level with building supplies. A screened top may be used over an ATBP, or the walls will need to be large enough to prevent the turtle from climbing out.

Lighting

Wild turtles bask in the sun to raise their core body temperature for proper digestion, immune function, and metabolism. They also use the UVB wavelengths of sunlight to make their needed vitamin D. Indoor turtles will need artificial lights to recreate their wild basking habits. Ideally, your slider's lights will be on timers so that the turtle gets 13 to 14 hours of light a day. Keeping a regular set time of 13 to 14 hours all year will help keep an indoor turtle awake, active, and eating during the winter. Never leave basking lights on 24 hours a day, as this can be very stressful. However, a nightlight in the room will not bother a turtle.

Heat Lights

An indoor slider will need a heat light over the basking spot, so that the basking spot reaches 85° to 90°F (29.4° to 32.2°C). This can be a simple dome fixture with a regular incandescent household light bulb screwed into the fixture. Dome light fixtures are commonly sold in pet stores, home improvement stores, and even some auto repair stores. The wattage of the bulb you need will depend on the size of the turtle and how close the basking spot is to the light. A 75-watt bulb would be a good one to start with. The wattage of the light or the height of the basking platform can be adjusted if it's too warm or too cold. It's best to avoid spot-light type bulbs, as they may concentrate heat into too small an area, which could result in health issues. A basking heat light *must* produce heat—the energy-saving compact florescent (CFL) bulbs do not produce enough heat.

If a turtle isn't basking, it could be that the basking platform is too cold compared to the water (if the water is warmer than the basking spot), or is too hot. A stressed turtle, such as one that was just added to a new enclosure, might also be hesitant to bask the first day or two.

UVB Lights

If your slider is kept outside, he'll get plenty of ultraviolet-B (UVB) light from natural sunlight. If he's kept indoors, however, he will need an artificial light to simulate the UVB rays of natural sunlight. A slider needs UVB to synthesize vitamin D_3, which is necessary for calcium absorption. Although a quality turtle pellet will contain vitamin D_3, it's still a good idea to use a UVB bulb in case the diet isn't perfect.

Most keepers use fluorescent bulbs that generate at least 5 percent UVB. Purchase one that is specifically made for use with reptiles. These bulbs must be within 12 inches (30.5 cm) of the

Enrichment

Some families add enrichment accessories to the tank to keep their turtle occupied during the day. A Ping-Pong ball can be floated in the water, and some turtles like to bat it around the tank. Even rubber duckies and tough teething rings for human babies have been used in turtle tanks. (Make sure all turtle items are marked so that they won't accidentally be used for anything other than the turtle tank.) Whatever you use, be sure that the turtle can't eat it or break off small parts, and that it is non-toxic. Switching old artificial plants for new ones will give the turtle something new to investigate. You can keep two or three additional plants on hand and rotate the plants periodically; that way you don't have to buy new ones every time you remove an old one. Although sliders suffer stress from large changes, such as a new enclosure, small changes such as a few new plants can enrich their lives.

Turtles seem to enjoy having caves, hollow logs, or other hiding places in their enclosure. Here is a painted turtle looking out from his safe spot.

basking spot to be effective, and they typically must be replaced every six to eight months, as their UVB output decreases over time. They also require a fixture to hold the fluorescent bulb.

Newer style mercury vapor bulbs on the market produce both heat and UVB light and can fit into a single dome fixture with a ceramic base. However, these lights were designed for large zoo enclosures and are very powerful. They can overheat delicate hatchlings, and they must be positioned farther away from the basking platform than a fluorescent UVB bulb. They should be at least 2 feet (61 cm) away from the basking platform.

Be aware that UVB doesn't pass through normal glass, including the glass used in windows and aquariums. If using a UVB bulb, it must not be housed behind a glass or plastic frame or your turtle will not receive the benefits of the lighting. Most aquarium fixtures for fluorescent bulbs have a plastic underside that must be removed if using a UVB bulb for your slider.

Lighting Placement
Light fixtures can be placed over a screen on top of a section of the enclosure, hung from the ceiling by chains, or clamped onto the side of the tank. No matter how the fixture is used, make certain that it cannot fall into the water or be knocked onto the floor. If it falls into the water, it may electrocute the turtle and blow a fuse. If it falls onto the floor, it may cause a fire if not found in time. For homes with indoor turtle enclosures and small children or cats, dome light fixtures can have two or three holes drilled into the bottom edge, and the dome fixture can then be

Live or Artificial Plants?

While live plants are fine as hide spots and look nice in a tank, sliders are prone to either digging up or eating all live plants in a tank. Small juveniles might appreciate anacharis in the water, or a piece or two of floating water hyacinth or water lettuce. Anacharis can be found in most pet stores while floating plants, occasionally available in pet stores, are most often found in plant nurseries. Some plants, such as parrot's feather and aquatic reeds, are less likely to be eaten, but there's no guarantee.

If you'd like to grow pond plants to add to your pet's diet, you can raise aquatic plants such as anacharis and water hyacinth in a separate container and add them to your turtle's enclosure periodically, letting the plants have time to propagate before being eaten. In a large pond you can make underwater plant corrals to keep turtles from eating expensive lilies, allowing you to keep turtles and plants in the same pond. If using pond plants, check into the legality of certain plants in your state. Water hyacinth and water fern are illegal in some states.

There are quite a variety of realistic artificial plants on the market now, and these will last much longer in a turtle enclosure than real ones. Silk plants are the most natural looking, but they can be a bit fragile. Plastic plants are more durable and also less expensive. Turtles don't seem to notice a difference between real and fake plants and will use whatever plants you provide for hiding and clinbing areas.

screwed onto the aquarium screen so that the heat light can't be tipped over.

Hiding Spot

All reptiles, especially hatchlings and juveniles, do better when they have access to hide spots. Hide spots make a turtle feel secure, resulting in improved psychological health, which is important for proper immune function. Stress exacerbates all illnesses, so the less stressed your slider is the healthier he likely will be. Basically, having a hide spot just makes a turtle feel better. Hatchlings in particular need hide spots, as they feel (rightfully so) that they are food for everything. If you have a bare tank, a juvenile is going to be highly stressed and less likely to eat.

Plants

Artificial silk or plastic plants are inexpensive but are attractive ways to create hide spots. They can be purchased from pet stores, dollar stores, craft stores, and even large general retail stores. Avoid plants with red, yellow, orange, or purple colors. Turtles can see color and might be tempted to sample a brightly colored artificial plant. Stick with green-colored artificial plants. There can be white, cream, or black in the background. These plants are especially helpful with juvenile turtles, which can hide and rest in the plants as well as bask on some of them, as they would in live aquatic plants in the wild. If using an egg crate basking platform or an above-tank basking platform, artificial plants can be zip-tied to the screen to float down into the water. In fact, artificial plants can be zip-tied to many different accessories in the tank, or they can be left free-floating in the tank.

If your silk plants develop ragged edges, remove them immediately. Turtles are inclined to nip at them when they're ragged, which could cause an intestinal impaction. Rarely a turtle will think that silk plants are edible. Watch the turtle closely after you add the plants. You should know within the first few minutes how the turtle reacts to his artificial plants.

Caves

Underwater caves add dimension to a habitat. Caves can be as fancy or simple as you like, store-bought or homemade. Always ensure that the turtle can turn around easily in one and won't get stuck as he grows. Pet stores and online catalogs sell hollow artificial floating basking logs that double as underwater hiding spots, but most sliders will eventually outgrow them. There are also artificial logs and stumps that look very realistic. Alternatively, you can make a simple underwater cave from a plastic shoe box or small tote with the lid still on the container. Remove one side from the container using a Dremel-style rotary tool or hot knife to avoid creating sharp edges that could injure your turtle. Attach a piece of slate or rock to the lid with aquarium sealant to hold the cave in place. If the tank is too small to accommodate an underwater hide spot, place an artificial plant in the water or have a solid basking

When setting up your slider's enclosure, make sure he can get in and out of the water easily.

platform that the turtle can rest under when he wants some time out.

Water Heater and Supplemental Heat

The water in a red-eared slider enclosure needs to be between 72° and 78°F (22.2° and 25.6°C), with hatchlings and younger juveniles being kept on the warmer end of the range. A sick turtle might need the temperature bumped up a few degrees, but try to keep the water below 85°F (29.4°C). If needed, you can use an aquarium heater to warm the water. Because sliders are active, inquisitive, and large, they may be able to break a glass heater, potentially leading to electrocution, cuts, or ingestion of glass pieces. Water heaters encased in special plastic covers are now available in most pet stores and are highly recommend for turtle aquariums. If you are using an older style glass heater, place it inside a PVC or ceramic

pipe of some sort with holes drilled in the pipe to allow for water flow.

Make sure to follow the instructions that come with the heater, as some heaters are designed to rest below the water level while some are designed to have the top of the heater above the water line. It's preferable to have one that's completely submersible. Some water heaters come with temperature settings, but use the manufacturer's settings only as a guide. Always use an independent water thermometer to check the water temperature, and adjust the setting on the heater if needed.

If the indoor air temperature at night is too cool—below about 68°F (20°C)—you can use a ceramic heat emitter (CHE) at night when the heat light is turned off. A CHE screws into a dome fixture just as an incandescent bulb does, but a CHE should be used only with light fixtures that have a ceramic base because they can melt plastic bases. Although some people prefer to use red or blue colored bulbs at night instead of ceramic heat emitters, some of the colored bulbs sold specifically for reptiles seem to burn out faster than regular light bulbs, and a CHE can last for years before needing to be replaced.

Thermometers

It's a good idea to have a water thermometer and an additional thermometer to gauge the temperature of the basking spot. Avoid the glass water thermometers typically sold for fish aquariums, as sliders might be attracted to the red fluid inside the glass and bite into the thermometer. If you must use a glass thermometer, place it in a PVC pipe or other spot that the turtle can't reach, or just hold it in place until you can get an accurate reading, then remove it from the tank.

You can also use a digital thermometer with an external probe or a temperature gun to measure the water and basking platform temperatures. A temperature gun is a handheld electrical device that allows you to point at an object and get an instant reading of the surface temperature. Most pet stores or online catalogs sell various thermometers, probes, and temperature guns.

Siphon

The water in a tank or pond eventually needs to be emptied out and replaced, no matter how good the filter. The easiest way to do this is with a siphon. A siphon can be a simple hose that drains into a bucket or bath tub or out of a window, or it can be a specially designed hose that attaches to a faucet for increased speed of draining and to add fresh water back to the tank. Such siphons come in different lengths and work well for up to 55- or 75-gallon (208.2- to 284-l) tanks. They do use a large amount of water. Also, if using a sink, you must disinfect the sink and countertops afterwards to

Beware of Escape Routes

Turtles are much better climbers than one might think. Basking platforms need to be covered to prevent escape, or be far enough from the top of the enclosure that a turtle stretching his front and back legs can't reach the top edge. Fences need to be tall enough— at least 2 feet (61 cm) tall—or smooth enough that a turtle can't climb them. Some sliders have been known to climb chain-link fences, chicken wire, and rough stone walls. If you keep your turtle outdoors, it's a good idea for the fence to have a cap along the top or be tilted slightly inward to prevent the turtle from climbing out. Turtles can also dig, so any outdoor fence needs to be buried at least 6 inches (15.2 cm) into the ground.

avoid a potential cross-contamination from the turtle tank to household surfaces. Some home improvement stores might sell similarly designed products for draining water beds, so check to see what's available locally or online.

For ponds and very large tanks, a utility pump, pond pump, or sump pump is the way to go. A utility pump can be purchased from almost any home improvement store. Utility pumps have a short hose that rests in the turtle's water and attaches to the utility pump's intake, while a longer hose runs the water from the pump. Be sure to follow the pump's instructions for use and maintenance; some may require the addition of a tablespoon or two of vegetable oil to the intake before each use. Pond and sump pumps are even easier, and can be dropped right into the water with a water hose attached to the outtake nozzle. A utility pump

is a good idea if you have several tanks and want to avoid cross-contamination between tanks, especially if keeping different species; each tank or pond can have its own intake hose. To prevent potential cross-contamination of native wildlife, never drain your tank into or near a native water source, such as a pond or creek.

Substrate

To use a substrate (material covering the bottom of the tank) or not and what type to use if you use one are hotly contested issues among turtle hobbyists. It's perfectly fine to keep an enclosure with a bare bottom; you don't need to have gravel or rocks in the bottom of the tank unless you use an undergravel filter as part of the filter system. Some keepers like the look of gravel in a tank, but it's not a necessity. Sliders will often eat gravel. It usually passes

Gravel is an acceptable substrate for a slider enclosure, although many hobbyists keep their turtles in bare-bottom tanks.

through without harm and turtles in the wild have been known to eat small rocks, so some experts feel it's better to keep gravel in a tank. On the other hand, a larger piece of gravel can cause an intestinal impaction, especially with juvenile turtles. Gravel can also trap dirt, making it harder to clean the tank. However, it may hide unsightly debris until you siphon out the water. So it's up to you to decide whether you want gravel in the bottom of the tank. Some keepers prefer to have large smooth river rocks on the bottom of the tank.

Whatever type of substrate you use—if you use one at all—make sure it is either too large for your turtle to eat or small enough that it won't cause an impaction if eaten. Avoid sand in an indoor slider tank, as sand can clog a filter and isn't needed for sliders.

Outdoor ponds can have a bare bottom with a plastic liner or concrete base, depending on the pond design. You can also have a rocky, muddy, or sandy bottom in your pond. If you use sand, only use play sand. Sand collected from beaches may be contaminated with salt, chemicals, or dangerous organisms.

Filtration

Every enclosure should have a filter of some kind. Turtles put out more waste than fish, so they need stronger filtration. Small in-the-tank or hang-over-the-rim filters will work for juvenile turtles or short-term display tanks, but adult turtles usually need something stronger. The only possible exception to needing a filter is a small enclosure used for short-term housing in which

One of the best filters for a turtle enclosure is a canister filter.

the water can be dumped from the container and filled from the sink or with a bucket on an as-needed basis.

No matter what type of filter you use, make sure that the turtle can't get a foot or tail stuck into the intake tube. A sponge filter, strainer, or small mesh cage should be attached to the intake tube to prevent turtle limbs from getting stuck.

How Filters Work

Filters can do more than just suck particles out of the water. They also can clean the water chemically. Aquarium filters use three types of filtration to keep your turtle's water clean: mechanical, biological, and chemical; some filters combine more than one type.

Mechanical filtration takes out the larger pieces of waste from the water

and prevents them from overloading the biological filtration. Some filters might have two forms of mechanical filtration: a pre-filter at the front of the intake tube will prevent especially large pieces of debris from clogging the pump, while a second mechanical filter in the filter unit handles smaller particles before the water moves on to be biologically filtered. Various types of plastic screen or foam mesh are used for mechanical filtration.

Biological filtration is accomplished by beneficial nitrifying bacteria that turn toxic nitrogen wastes into less harmful compounds. Bacteria will colonize the nooks and crannies in biomedia such as bioballs, lava rock, foam pads, and various other media. The more area that a medium has for bacteria to live on, the better it works. This is why lava rock is such a good biological filter media—all the little holes provide more room for the bacteria. The more biomedia in a filter, the better it performs. However,

more media might require a stronger pump, and it will weigh more, which is something to take into consideration when choosing media and cleaning the filter unit. Biomedia can be placed in a mesh bag to make it easier to clean the filter. If you're not pleased with the biomedia that came with a purchased filter, you can mix and match biomedia to fit your needs.

It takes time for bacteria to colonize media, so if possible set up your tank and filter before acquiring a turtle. This will give the filter time to cycle and build up beneficial bacteria. Otherwise, your tank may be cloudy for up to two weeks if you add a filter after adding the turtle. If you're buying a new filter to replace an old one, let the two run concurrently for some time so that the new filter has time to build up bacteria before the old one is removed. If using a filter, always use dechlorinated water to fill the tank so that the chlorine doesn't deplete the beneficial bacteria. Most pet stores

Cleaning the Aquarium

Water changes and cleaning the tank can be time-consuming. However, some keepers make it harder than it needs to be, feeling that they must take apart every aspect of the aquarium and wash the interior. You don't have to scrub down all accessories or the tank every time you change the water. On a regular basis, as the quality of the water in the tank dictates— probably once a week to once a month depending on your tank size and filter's ability to filter the water— siphon out the water. Rinse off the walls or use a paper towel to go over the sides of the tank. If using gravel, you can mix up the gravel as you siphon the water to stir up debris and siphon it out. Replace the water in the tank with dechlorinated water. Take apart the filter and rinse the media in old aquarium water or dechlorinated water, then re-assemble and start the filter again.

That's all you need to do for the regular cleaning of the tank. There's no need to remove all of the substrate, decorations, or artificial plants. If they seen dirty or grimy, you can rinse them off, but there's really no need to disinfect them on a regular basis. If algae or hardwater stains are building up on the inner walls of an aquarium, remove them periodically with a razor blade. Although some people don't like the look of algae on basking spots, accessories, or tank walls, it doesn't hurt anything.

sell dechlorinator that can be added to the water before you add it to the tank. Always rinse new biological filtration media to remove dust before using them in a filter.

A third component of filtration is chemical filtration, usually accomplished by activated carbon that removes dissolved contaminants from the water. Some turtle filter systems use chemical filtration and some don't. Usually activated carbon is placed in a mesh bag before being added to a filter, and most commercially available canister-type filters have an area for the carbon. Rinse the carbon thoroughly with water before use, as it is very dusty. This is true even for the pre-made carbon packets sold with smaller filter systems—always rinse a new packet well before adding it to a filter. Because turtles produce such a large amount of waste, activated carbon is depleted relatively quickly. It might be useful for the first week or two that a filter is operating, while bacteria are building up, but you can remove it once the filter is working well.

Canister Filters

For aquariums, canister filters are the preferred filtration for several reasons. They hold more filter media than in-tank or on-the-tank filters; they can be placed out of sight below a tank; and they're usually quieter than on-the-tank filters. Canister filters also have intake and outtake hoses that can be placed at opposite sides of the tank for better water flow. Try to get a bit more powerful filter than your tank

size indicates. For example, if you have a 5-inch (12.7-cm) slider in a 55-gallon (208.2-l) tank, it doesn't hurt to get a filter rated for a 75- or 90-gallon (284- or 340.7-l) tank. Some of the new models are self-priming; others will require you to pour water into the intake tube to start the water flowing before the filter is turned on. Always read and save the manufacturer's instructions. If you've purchased a secondhand filter, most manufacturers have instructions online, and some even have instructional videos on their websites. Large canister filters can be frustrating for first-time users, and they're a bit pricey, but once you get the knack of it, you'll wonder how you ever lived without one.

Dual Filtration Systems

Some keepers swear by a dual filtration system created by using an undergravel filter connected to the intake line of a canister filter. Undergravel filters have been used in small aquariums for decades and can be found in any pet store. In theory, these filters circulate water through the gravel, where healthy bacteria grow and break down waste. However, an undergravel system isn't powerful enough to handle the waste that a turtle produces. When combined with a canister filter, though, the undergravel filter acts as a pre-filter and biological filter for the more powerful canister filter. However, some hobbyists feel that gravel shouldn't be used with turtles in a captive environment, so you'll have to investigate the alternatives to decide whether this system will work

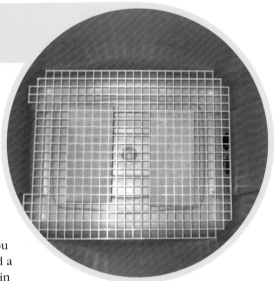

Egg crate frame in the tote filter. This forms the base for the rest of the filter media.

for you. It would be possible to use larger gravel that the turtle couldn't ingest, but that may weaken the effectiveness of an undergravel/canister filter system. You'll need at least 3 inches (7.6 cm) of gravel if you choose to use this combination.

Making Your Own Filter

For ponds and large aquariums, you can use a homemade filter—called a tote filter—with a pond pump or in addition to a canister filter. To build a simple basic tote filter, you will need:

- a plastic container such as tote or bucket
- a drill or other tool to make holes in the container
- biological filter media, such as bioballs or lava rock
- mesh bags to hold biomedia (optional)
- mechanical filter media, such as foam or mesh pads
- plastic egg crate screen
- flexible tubing designed for pond pumps (the size will depend on your pump outlets)
- 2 bricks
- a pond pump
- a pre-filter for the pump (optional)

If not using a pre-filter, you'll need

something to prevent the turtle from coming into contact with the intake section of the pump, such as a plastic strainer, wire mesh, or a cage made from plastic egg crate or a modified milk crate, depending on the size of your turtles.

To assemble the filter, do the following:

1. Drill or otherwise pierce one or two holes into the center of one side of the plastic tote, about an inch (2.5 cm) or so from the bottom of the container. The filtered water will exit from these holes.

2. Drill another hole about 3 to 4 inches (7.6 to 10.2 cm) from the top of the container to serve as an overflow outlet if the filter becomes clogged.

3. If using a lid for the container, drill a hole in the center of the lid. The hole in the lid should be

What a Slider Needs

Almost completed filter, showing the biological media—lava rock and bioballs—and the furnace filter covering it.

just barely larger than the outtake tubing from the pump.

4. Cut a piece of egg crate screen to just fit into the bottom of the container.

5. Place two bricks on the bottom of the container and position the egg crate over the bricks. The egg crate will prevent filter media from clogging the water flow through the holes in the plastic container.

6. Add 2 to 4 inches (5 to 10.2 cm) of biological media such as bio-balls or lava rock. Keep the weight of the material in mind. You don't want the filter so heavy that you can't move it for cleaning and maintenance. Other types of biological media might include plastic mesh pot scrubbers (brand new of course), Bio-Glass, and Crystal Bio. Crystal Bio is made from superheated glass, a process that creates air pockets that beneficial bacteria can colonize. It is lighter in weight than lava rock and has up to ten times more surface area than most plastic biomedia.

7. Cut the foam or mesh filter to fit over the biomedia so that 2 to 4 inches (5 to 10.2 cm) of foam or mesh covers the biomedia completely. Plastic mesh furnace filters are excellent for this, and less expensive then filter material sold specifically for ponds. Make sure the filter media you buy is made of plastic, not fiberglass, as fiberglass is harmful if inhaled or ingested.

8. Add the layers of the mechanical filter media (foam or mesh material) over the biological media.

9. Add the lid, if using one. Insert the tubing from the outflow of a canister filter or pond pump into the lid of the tote, and your filter is complete! You may want to use bricks to weigh down the tubing where it is inserted into the top of the tote, or use a clamp of some kind if not using a lid.

If used outdoors, the tote filter can sit at the edge of a rock ledge so that the water trickles out of the lower side hole(s) directly into the pond. If you prefer to direct the flow of the water to a specific area of the pond rather than just letting if flow directly from the hole(s) in the filter, place tubing in the bottom hole(s) and seal the edges of the hole(s) with epoxy.

You can use bricks to weigh down the intake hose and keep it in place.

If the tote filter is for an aquarium or indoor pond, a simple frame can be placed over one end of the tank so that the filter rests over the tank and drains directly into the tank. The frame can be as simple as two boards cut to extend over both sides of the tank. It's recommended that the boards be sealed with paint or epoxy so that they don't mold from the high humidity the filter will create. PVC pipe of the appropriate diameter can also be used to hold a tote filter, although heavier filters might need PVC pipe reinforced with metal pipe inside. For an indoor pond, a frame made from a milk crate or similar items can be used to hold the tote filter above the water line inside of the pond.

If you have all of your materials and tools available when you start, it will take less than an hour to make this filter, and it will cost much less

than a store-bought filter. There's no substitute for proper water filtration, and a good pump and filter will save hours of labor.

Cleaning and Maintenance

Filters need to be cleaned weekly to monthly, depending on the type of filter and how much waste is being filtered. It's best to rinse the filter media in a bucket with aquarium water or dechlorinated water so that the beneficial bacteria aren't killed by chlorine in tap water. However, if a filter has been a bit too long between cleanings, it's acceptable to rinse it with a high-powered hose. Filter media that's especially clogged can be rinsed in tap water to remove the majority of the waste, then soaked in 3 percent hydrogen peroxide for an hour or so, then rinsed and flushed with tap water. This will kill off the beneficial bacteria

in the filter, which will take time to build back up before the filter can run at peak efficiency again, but it can extend the life of clogged filter media.

Water Testing Kit

Although not an absolute necessity, it's recommended that keepers use a water quality testing kit to measure the ammonia, nitrate, and nitrite levels of the water. You can use any number of water testing kits sold at pet stores for aquarium use. Clear water is not always an indication of clean water, and a test kit can help you determine the levels of waste in the water. If you have a high-performing filter and your water quality test shows the water is clean, you may only have to top off the water level of the enclosure that is lost to evaporation. If the ammonia and other waste levels are high, you must siphon the water, replace with fresh

Completed filter in use.

This large indoor pond is built around a plastic stock tank. Homemade enclosures can be as decorative as you like as long as they provide your turtle with a suitable habitat.

dechlorinated water, and clean the filter. If the water quality is consistently poor, then it might be time to upgrade to a new or additional filter.

Egg-Laying Area

If you have an adult female, she may at some time need to lay eggs, even if she's never been with a male. Although some turtles aren't too picky about where they lay eggs, and may just drop the eggs in the water of the aquarium, many females will want to dig a nest to lay their eggs. These females can develop health problems if they don't have an area to lay eggs.

An indoor nesting box needs to be deep enough to hold roughly 8 to 12 inches (20.3 to 30.5 cm) of substrate and be 18 inches (45.7 cm) in length and width. A turtle won't like hitting the side or bottom of a container with her hind feet while she's digging; she'll think she's hitting a rock and try to dig another nest. The substrate can be a mixture of slightly damp play sand and peat moss or play sand and top soil. Play sand is designed to be safe for children playing in a sand box, so make sure you're purchasing play sand and not another type of sand.

You can make a simple nesting box from a plastic tote with a ramp leading up from the water of the enclosure. If you have a frame or cap built over one end of an aquarium or indoor pond, you can set the tote on a stand next to the enclosure so that it doesn't take up any water space. Just make sure your turtle can't escape from the ramp or nesting area out of the enclosure. In some cases, if you don't have room to put a nesting box in the enclosure or next to it, the turtle can be placed into a large tote with deeper substrate during the day, then put back into the water enclosure at night.

Check the substrate for eggs each day until you find eggs. If you're fairly certain that your turtle has eggs but she hasn't laid them for over a week, it might be a good time for a vet visit.

If you have a pond in an enclosed yard, your turtle will probably wander around looking for just the right spot. You can help by loosening one patch of soil in the yard or enclosure. Make the egg-laying patch about 12 inches (30.5 cm) deep and 18 (45.7 cm) long and wide and adding some sand to the soil. Try to pick a sunny spot that's free of vegetation. Your turtle may surprise you, though, and decide to lay eggs in a mulch pile or flower bed.

Ponds

Ponds come in many types, from preformed or lined to large stock tanks sunk into the ground. A pond offers a slider unparalleled living space and water volume.

Indoor Ponds

You can purchase or make an indoor pond. A simple wooden frame can be made from boards and then lined with 45 mil EPDM (ethylene propylene diene monomer) pond liner. It's best to have a cap between the frame and liner to keep turtles in and to stabilize the liner, as well as for aesthetics. Make sure you're getting EPDM liner made for ponds, as EPDM is also made for roofing material and roofing EPDM may have algicides and fire retardants that can be deadly to turtles and fish. EPDM material can be found at many home improvement stores or plant nurseries.

You can make basking spots for ponds similarly to the way you would make them in aquariums. Also, a very simple basking area can be made by placing bag of mulch, an old laundry basket, or something appropriately sized under one corner of the liner, although this will reduce the water volume. Heat lights and UVB lights may be hung from the ceiling with chains if you'd like an unobstructed view of the turtles, or you can make frames to hold the lighting.

If you have especially large and heavy turtles, such as large adult female sliders or cooters, you can cover the basking area with a thick rubber stall mat

Drowning

Ensure that your slider can move freely in his tank and can't get stuck behind basking platforms or heavy hide spots. Despite the fact that sliders live in the water, there is still a risk that they'll drown if they get stuck under water. Some keepers have reported older juveniles getting stuck between a floating turtle dock and the glass of an aquarium or between a heavy filter and the side of the enclosure, resulting in the drowning of the turtle. Strong intake suction from a filter can also trap a young or weak turtle under the water.

If you keep multiple turtles in one enclosure, it is best to have multiple basking platforms—although the turtles may still pile up in one spot.

designed for horse stalls. This prevents the claws of these heavy turtles from digging into the liner and puncturing it when the turtle climbs up to the basking spot. Agriculture supply stores such as Tractor Supply Co., Southern States, True Value, and online catalogs may carry stall mats.

Outdoor Ponds

Although outdoor ponds won't be covered in depth here, there are many books, magazines, and online resources for constructing and maintaining a pond. Home improvement and garden supply stores will have all of the materials you need and may be able to offer expert advice.

Outdoor ponds must be deep enough to prevent the water from overheating in the summer and to prevent complete freezing in the winter. If keeping a slider outside, it's recommended that the pond be at

least 300 gallons (1135.6 l) to allow for proper temperature regulation. Some keepers prefer to use a floating deicer in the winter as well. Ideally, outdoor ponds will be screened in or built inside a screened frame to keep out predators such as raccoons, herons, and eagles.

If considering an outdoor pond, think carefully about the location. Consider how close it is to outdoor electrical outlets and how you'll get electricity to the filter. A pond should get partial shade or be covered partially with a shade cloth, although a pond directly under a tree will get too much debris with fallen leaves and the like. A pond shouldn't be at the lowest part of the yard, as the water pressure at the bottom of a hill can actually push up on a pond liner and invert it, dislodging the water. Check the location of buried power lines and water and sewer pipes to make sure you won't disturb them

52

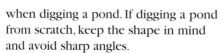

when digging a pond. If digging a pond from scratch, keep the shape in mind and avoid sharp angles.

If you allow a slider to hibernate outside during the winter, the pond bottom must be dug below the frost line to prevent freezing in the winter. The frost line is the depth to which the groundwater in soil is expected to freeze. Most garden centers and university agricultural centers will know the frost line for your area, and it is often written into local building codes. If the bottom of your pond isn't dug below the frost line, the entire pond may freeze in the winter, which will kill a hibernating turtle. Even if you don't let your sliders hibernate outside, it's still a good idea to dig the pond deep enough to keep liners from cracking during freezing. Consider renting a backhoe and driver to dig the hole, as it is a time-consuming task to dig

a hole with shovels.

If using shelves for potted aquatic plants, either remove the plants before winter starts or place the pots at the bottom of the pond for winter storage. A slider may attempt to hibernate in a potted plant, and if the pot is in shallow water the turtle could freeze during hibernation.

Safety

Always keep safety in mind when keeping turtles and aquariums. Electrical cords from lights and filters should have a drip loop between the tank and electrical outlet. This means that a cord or wire doesn't travel in a straight line from the appliance to the outlet; rather, the cord hangs down and then loops back up before reaching the outlet. This way, if water gets on the cord, it will run down to the loop and drip onto the floor rather than running into the outlet. If the cord goes all the way to the ground, make sure it is covered or secured so that it can't be stepped on. A cord that is constantly underfoot can become frayed and be a fire hazard and well as be tripped over, resulting in injuries or fire hazard if the cord is pulled and a lamp falls over.

Use ground fault circuit interrupters (GFCI) for all outdoor enclosures. A GFCI is an electrical wiring device that interrupts a circuit whenever it detects an imbalance in the electric current. It can prevent an electrical shock if a piece of electrical equipment malfunctions.

If using extension cords or power strips, make sure they are rated for the appropriate wattage of your pumps and lights. Place them out of the way to keep them from becoming tripping hazards.

Predators

If you keep your slider outside, be aware of outdoor predators. Hatchlings and juveniles are at risk from wading birds, such as herons, and even crows and other birds. Large fish (such as ornamental koi commonly kept in backyard ponds) and large bullfrogs are other threats, and even some snakes will eat hatchling turtles. Surprisingly, bald eagles hunt turtles in the wild, as do other birds of prey. Raccoons, skunks, coyotes, and opossums can also hunt and eat turtles. Raccoons are especially a problem for turtles and can fish them out of a typical backyard pond. Many keepers build their ponds specifically to be raccoon proof, with the pond dug deeper than would be typical, so the water level can start at least a foot below the ground level, and a rock ledge that extends farther over the water than is typical. This type of pond would be good for male sliders, although it could be acceptable for females if an egg-laying area or island is made in the center of the pond. Curious children have been known to walk off with a neighbor's turtle, too.

Water lilies make a pond beautiful and provide hiding and resting areas for your turtle.

To keep predators out, consider installing an electric fence around the pond, or enclosing the entire pond area in a lockable screened-in frame. For smaller turtles, some keepers use deer netting over the pond to keep out birds. If possible, keep a lock on all yard gates to keep out intruders.

Turtles and Other Animals

Although sliders and other emydids have a hard shell to hide in, they are often seen as food or toys by other animals. Dogs, no matter how friendly or how small, should never be left alone with turtles. The same is true for pet ferrets and rats, which all see turtles as a potential food source. If your pond area is accessible to dogs, always monitor your dog's activities around the pond. Turtles may occasionally leave the pond to wander the yard, so don't assume that the turtle is safe in the pond. Some dogs have even been known to retrieve turtles out of the pond. Cats might be curious about a turtle and could stick a paw into the tank, which could result in the cat having

Unplug the Heater

When changing the water, *always* unplug the heater before draining the water. If a filter has been sitting outside the water while turned on and then you add new water, it will break.

a nipped paw. Cats may also knock over any unsecured heat lights.

Keeping a Slider with Other Turtles

Keep in mind that sliders can be aggressive with other turtles once they reach adult size. Even two females from the same clutch that have been raised together from hatchlings may not get along in a captive environment once they reach breeding age (at roughly 6 to 7 inches [15.2 to 17.8 cm]). Turtles, especially sliders, are very individualistic animals; some do well with other turtles and some do not. If you decide to keep two sliders together, regardless of the sex of either turtle, there's always a chance they will eventually have to be separated permanently. A larger enclosure might tip the scales in favor of a group of sliders coexisting, but that's never a guarantee. If you do keep two or more turtles together, remember the 10-gallon (38-l) rule of thumb: turtles need roughly 10 gallons per inch (38 l per 2.5 cm) of turtle shell. So two adults of either sex would need at least a 100-gallon (378.5-l) tank, although larger is always better.

Never keep two turtles of drastically different sizes in the same enclosure. Adult turtles may see hatchlings as food, and larger turtles can injure smaller ones. Although adults of different sizes can be kept together if they get along and there's enough space, it's best to keep juveniles and adults separate from each other.

In addition, some other species do better or worse with sliders. Cooters

Turtles climb better than you probably would imagine, so be sure yours does not have a way to climb up and out of the enclosure.

and redbellies get huge—2 to 4 inches (5 to 10.2 cm) larger than red-eared sliders—but they tend to be very peaceful species that get along with most other turtles. Remember that there are always exceptions, and there's no guarantee the slider will get along with a redbelly. Male painteds, on the other hand, are often exceptionally aggressive with females of any species, and it's best to keep them separate from any female in a captive environment, unless in an extremely large pond.

Think long and hard before bringing home another turtle, and always be prepared for the worst case scenario should they have to be separated into two different enclosures. If you do bring in another turtle, he should go through a quarantine period in a separate enclosure to make sure he's healthy before being added to the same enclosure as your current pet(s). Some experts say this should be six months, but some feel that two months is acceptable. If the turtle is coming from a trusted source, such as a rescue or hobbyist who has had him for some time by himself, it might be acceptable to forgo quarantine.

Turtles With Fish and Frogs

Although many keepers like to keep fish with turtles, this can be a double-edged sword. Many fish end up being food for a turtle. On the other hand, some feeder fish might go uneaten and grow into permanent tankmates. In a pond, turtles generally ignore koi and large goldfish, although turtles may eat a weak or sick fish and often will nip at fins. If there are especially large koi in a pond, the larger, more aggressive fish might eat most of the food, resulting in an underfed turtle that cannot survive

What a Slider Needs

hibernation. If keeping fish in your pond, pay attention at feeding time to ensure that your slider is getting his share of the food.

Indoor turtles should never be kept with frogs or other amphibians. A

captive frog would quickly end up as a turtle's dinner. Some amphibians also excrete toxic substances that could be harmful to a slider. Frogs and tadpoles in a backyard pond may or may not be eaten by a resident turtle.

Disinfecting Enclosures

Tubing, basking sites, and other accessories will need to be disinfected or otherwise cleaned from time to time. Surfaces used to clean up after your slider, such as bathroom sinks and countertops, also need to be disinfected afterward. If you purchased used equipment, such as a secondhand aquarium, you'll want to disinfect it before using it with your pet.

Clean it First

Start by scrubbing all dirt, scum, or other debris from the equipment and rinsing it well before using a disinfectant. Do this because dirt and organic material decrease the effectiveness of most disinfectants. You can use a mild soap to scrub surfaces, but *all* traces of soap must be rinsed away. If you doubt that you can completely remove soap residue, forgo the soap, but make sure that all dirt is scrubbed and rinsed away before using a disinfectant.

If you need to remove dirt or scum from a hard-to-reach area, such as the inside of tubing, 3-percent hydrogen peroxide can be used to rinse the tubing. Let it sit for five to ten minutes, then rinse thoroughly before disinfecting.

Disinfection

Bleach is very inexpensive and is readily available at any grocery store, but it can

FAMILY-FRIENDLY TIP

Kids and Cleaning Chores

It's probably not a good idea to have younger children help with cleaning the filter, as this can be a messy job. Younger children may get aquarium water on areas that can't be disinfected properly. However, younger children can be given a check list to go over each time the tank is cleaned so that they can check off everything that needs to be done and help remind an older sibling or adult of what needs to be done, such as adding dechlorinator and checking to make sure all filter hoses are secure. Older children can help rinse artificial plants and accessories and refill the tank with water. If using a water testing kit weekly, children can dip the testing stick in a water sample and help read the results. Always make sure your kids wash their hands after coming in contact with turtles or their water.

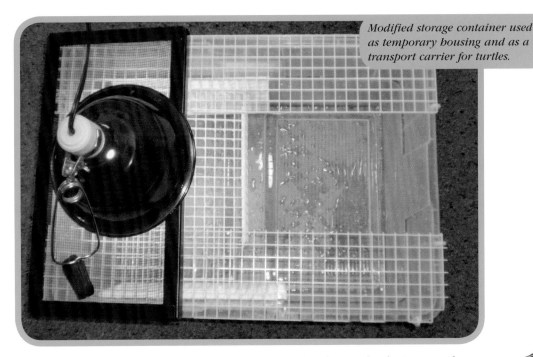

discolor clothing and carpet. It can also pit and damage stainless steel and other metals, so check on the components of filters and screens before disinfecting them with bleach. Use bleach only in a well ventilated room, as the fumes can be harsh. A 10-percent bleach solution— one part bleach to nine parts water—is ideal for killing most bacteria, mold, and viruses if allowed to have contact with a surface for at least ten minutes. A spray bottle full of the bleach solution can be used to saturate all surfaces, and a pan full can be used to soak tubing or small cage accessories. After ten minutes contact time with bleach, rinse well. If possible, let the disinfected items sit out in the sun for a day before use, or rinse all items with water containing a dechlorinator. If using a bleach solution to soak ceramics or a rock substrate, let the items soak in dechlorinated water overnight after rinsing them and before adding them to the enclosure.

Bleach does have a shelf life, and an unopened bottle should be discarded if over a year old. A bottle of bleach should be discarded within two months of opening the bottle. Diluted bleach should be discarded after 24 hours. *Never* mix ammonia with bleach, because this will create toxic fumes. Never use bleach at full strength.

Chlorhexidine is an antibacterial and antifungal cleaner that is commonly used in dairies and veterinary clinics. It is available under a few brand names. It can be purchased from farm supply stores, some veterinarians, or on-line agricultural supply catalogs. Use

chlorhexidine in 1:50 dilution with water. Although chlorhexidine is not as available as bleach, it has no toxic fumes and isn't affected by organic materials as much as bleach is. Never use chlorhexidine at full strength.

Never use phenolic household cleaners, such as Pine-Sol or Lysol, on turtle accessories, because phenols may be toxic to reptiles.

Transporting Your Slider

Many people are confused when it comes to transporting a turtle. How do you travel with an animal that usually lives in the water? The answer is both a little surprising and very simple.

Never carry your slider in a container of water during transport or travel. The sloshing back and forth could cause your turtle to accidentally inhale, or aspirate, water into his or her lungs. This can lead to pneumonia or other infections. Also, if the water is

too deep and the turtle is in a container for a long period, it is possible for the turtle to become tired and drown if there's no place to rest. This is especially true of hatchlings.

Turtles need something absorbent to soak up waste and something to cover them to make them feel secure during transport. A good rule of thumb is to transport turtles under 4 inches (10.2 cm) in shell length in a damp substrate, such as damp paper towels or sphagnum moss. The substrate should feel damp to the touch but shouldn't be dripping wet. Dampened shredded newspaper will work in a pinch, too. Just rip the newspaper into long strips by hand. Long-fiber sphagnum moss is especially good for hatchlings, as they can bury themselves in it to feel secure and still be in a humid environment. It's a little expensive, but can be found in many home improvement stores and plant nurseries.

Larger turtles can rest in dry shredded newspaper or a towel. Don't use shredded copy or printing paper, as that could have sharp edges. It's especially important that larger and heavier turtles, such as adult female sliders and redbellies, have a layer of padding under them when transported. Large turtles are usually heavy enough that they can bruise their plastron during transport if there's not enough padding under them. An extra towel or a piece of foam rubber can go on the bottom of the container for the larger turtles, in addition to an absorbent material. A thick layer of fluffed, shredded newspaper or a towel can cover and cushion the turtle on the top and sides.

Plastic totes, shoeboxes, and even small plastic food containers are useful for transport, depending on the size of the turtle. If you use a plastic container to hold or transport a turtle, use a permanent marker to label it for turtle use only so that is doesn't get mixed up with other household items. Use a hot knife or a drill to add numerous air holes to the sides of the container. Make sure there are no sharp edges on the inside of the container.

For a short trip to the veterinarian, larger turtles can travel in a cardboard box with a few air holes added on the sides. Just be sure the lid on any travel container is secure—you may have to tape the lid down—and that the bottom has enough absorbent material so that it isn't weakened if it becomes wet.

When traveling, make sure the enclosure isn't in direct sunlight. A turtle can overheat quickly in direct sunlight. In especially hot or cold weather, it may be necessary to double box the turtle with an outer box containing a Styrofoam box with air holes added. If it's especially cold outside, the turtle can be double boxed with a heat pack placed between the two containers.

If you're traveling across country, such as when moving, use a larger plastic tote for transport and for housing on a short-term basis. For example, if a 6-inch (15.2-cm) male slider is moving with the family in a car, he can stay in the back seat or on the floor (out of direct sunlight) of the car in a 44-quart (41.6-l) plastic bin with shredded newspaper during the day. At night, when stopping over at a hotel or relative's house, throw out the newspaper and add a few inches (4 cm or so) of water to the bin to allow the turtle to drink and eat overnight. A turtle might not eat for a few days due to the stress of travel. If the basking spot is small enough to fit into the enclosure, put it into the enclosure when you add the water. A screen over one end can hold a heat light over the basking area, but don't leave the light on all night. The next day, dump the water, remove the basking area, and add fresh newspaper. If this is for a household move, the bin or tote can be used as temporary housing for a few days until the permanent enclosure arrives with the rest of the household shipment.

Chapter 3

What a Slider

Eats

Red-eared sliders are true opportunistic omnivores.
In the wild they eat a wide variety of foods,
including aquatic plants, fish, insects, freshwater
clams and other mollusks, and even carrion.
In captivity they can be conveniently fed on
commercial turtle pellets, but variety is the spice
of life for any animal. Pellets should be the staple
of the diet, with dark leafy greens and vegetables
and/or aquatic plants being regular additions.
Fruits and animal protein of various forms can be
used as treats.

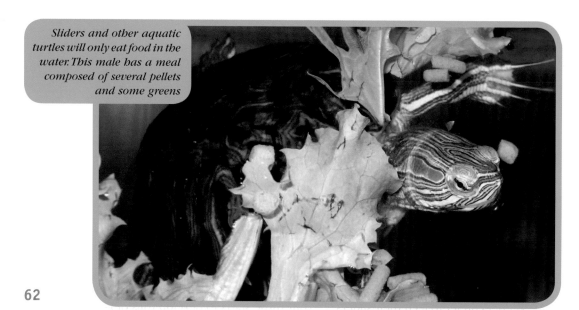

Sliders and other aquatic turtles will only eat food in the water. This male has a meal composed of several pellets and some greens

Feeding a Slider

Sliders and other aquatic turtles eat only while they're in the water, so all foods must be placed in the water. Hatchling turtles should be fed daily. Sliders that are roughly 3 to 5 inches (7.6 to 12.7 cm) can be fed every other day. Very large adults need feeding only three times a week. Offer an amount of pellets roughly the size of the turtle's head or the amount that the turtle can eat in 15 minutes. You can offer greens at any time. Treats of fruits, vegetables, and animal protein (earthworms, for example) can be given two or three times a week.

Offering more pelleted or soft food than a turtle can consume in 15 to 30 minutes can cause the water to become dirty very quickly. Try to judge what your turtle will eat within that time and go from there. Greens and hard vegetables, such as sweet potato, or harder fruits, such as apple, can last a big longer in the tank, but if they aren't eaten after a few hours, remove them from the tank to keep the enclosure clean.

Turtles are great at begging, so they may always seem hungry. If you must give in to their begging, offer a piece of some leafy green. It might help to offer food at the same time of day every day that the turtle is fed; that might make him less likely to beg at other times.

Feeding New Sliders

Don't be surprised if your new pet doesn't eat for the first day or two after you bring him home. Stressed reptiles often refuse to eat for the first few days. If you need something to jump-start the appetite of a stressed turtle, try some animal protein such as a piece of cooked shrimp or a live insect. If he hasn't eaten for more than a week, though, there could be an underlying health or husbandry problem.

For hatchling turtles that won't eat, try frozen bloodworms (the larvae of a midge) or mosquito larvae, sold in little packs (dry or frozen) in the fish food section of many pet stores. Small crickets and pieces of earthworms are often readily accepted by stressed-out newly acquired turtles. Try crickets as a last resort, though, due to the risk of nematode infection from crickets.

Feeding in a Separate Container

Because turtles can be messy eaters, some keepers prefer to feed their sliders in a separate container. This keeps the primary aquarium or tank water cleaner, although that is not a necessity. A feeding container can be a dish pan reserved for this purpose or a plastic shoe box or tote. Place a few inches (7 cm or so) of water in the container (the volume depends on the size of the turtle). Then add the turtle and the food. After half an hour or so, put the turtle back into his regular enclosure and discard the waste water in the feeding enclosure—flushing it down the toilet usually works.

Make sure the turtle can't climb out of his feeding container or that other household pets can't get into it. Some turtles may find the short-term move stressful and refuse to eat at first. If you have artificial plants in the primary enclosure, you can add some of them to the feeding container at feeding time so that the turtle has something familiar in the container to hide under. This will help him feel more comfortable in the feeding container. Once he's eating regularly, you won't have to add the plants. If you've just brought home your new turtle, give him a few days or weeks to adjust to his new home before trying a separate feeding container—you don't want too much stress too soon. You don't have to use a separate feeding container, but some people prefer to do so, and some use it when housing multiple turtles to make sure each turtle is getting his or her fair share of the food.

Overfeeding and Underfeeding

It is possible to overfeed a turtle. If your turtle starts to develop rolls of fat

63

FAMILY-FRIENDLY TIP

Let's Do It Together

Most children enjoy feeding pets, including turtles. You need to find age-appropriate tasks for your kids, so they can both have fun and help out with feeding time. Younger children can wash greens and vegetables and measure the pellets. Older children can peel carrots and sweet potatoes, and cut or break larger vegetables such as carrots and squashes into more manageable pieces. This is a good time to explain the importance of variety in a diet for turtles and people!

What a Slider Eats

Dandelion flowers and greens make excellent food for red-eared slider. They are high in calcium and vitamin A.

between the hind legs and shell, reduce the amount of food that you offer each time. On the other hand, if the hip bones between the tail and hind legs become apparent, you need to increase the amount or frequency of your feedings, or check with a veterinarian to see whether there's an underlying health issue. You can use a gram scale to weigh your turtle weekly if want to monitor his weight closely. Gram scales should be fine for juveniles, most males, and younger females. Some scales designed for weighing people might be able to measure the weight of larger sliders over 2 pounds (0.9 kg).

Foods for Sliders

Some foods are okay to feed only as long as they are not a frequent or large part of the diet. For example, spinach, parsley, carrots, and chard contain chemicals called oxalates, which interferes with calcium absorption. *Brassica* vegetables such as kale, broccoli, Brussels sprouts, cauliflower, and cabbage (also known as cruciferous vegetables) contain goitrogenic compounds that reduce iodine absorption, which leads to impairment of thyroid gland function. However, all of these foods also contain excellent levels of vitamins A, C, and K, and other important nutrients such as calcium, iron, antioxidants, and anticancer compounds. Therefore, offering them in small quantities as part of a varied diet can prevent them from causing health problems while still giving your pet quality nutrition and something interesting in the diet. There are some foods that you should never feed a turtle, and those are discussed later in this chapter.

You might see warnings about iceberg lettuce, as it has little nutritional value. However, it won't hurt your turtle if he has a leaf of iceberg lettuce every now and again, so long as the rest of his diet is complete. Almost any food can be used as the occasional treat. Just don't give in to begging. A slider would eat almost every hour of every day if allowed, and it is possible for a turtle to eat too much.

Pellets

Commercially prepared pelleted foods should be the staple of any slider diet. You can use those made specifically for aquatic turtles or use those intended for trout or koi. If available, pellets made for crocodilians are great for adult sliders—most brands come in different sizes, so make sure the size of the pellet matches the size of the turtle. Pelleted foods labeled as "sticks" are usually great for hatchlings, as they soften fairly quickly in the water.

If you purchase large quantities of commercial food, check for expiration dates on packages. Divide the food into small equal portions in airtight plastic bags or containers and store them in a cool dark place until needed. Bulk pelleted food can usually be stored in a refrigerator or freezer for up to six months in airtight containers. Commercial pellets contain fat that can go rancid over time, and vitamins can degrade as well, especially if exposed to light over time. Some keepers form a food co-op with other turtle enthusiasts so that a large bag of food can be purchased at a discount rate and then divided between several keepers.

Vegetables

You can feed your slider almost any item you find in the produce department. Leafy greens are excellent; these include romaine lettuce, dandelion, kale, collard greens, turnip greens, mustard greens, escarole (an endive), and spring lettuce mixes. Just let the greens float on top of the water. Other good vegetables for your turtle include carrots, sweet potatoes,

Several backyard weeds make great slider food. Wild plantain is one that is common and easy to identify.

Aquatic Plants

Sliders feed heavily on aquatic plants, and you can find several appropriate varieties at pet stores and home and garden supply stores. Here is a small selection of commonly available species. Remove any snails on the plants before feeding them to your slider. This helps prevent transmitting parasites to your turtle.

Anacharis

Parrot's feather

Water hyacinth

Water lettuce

summer and winter squashes, fresh pumpkin, green beans, and broccoli. Wash all vegetables well, as you would if eating them yourself. Thinly slice or grate hard vegetables such as carrots, sweet potatoes, and winter squashes. Larger turtles can eat larger slices or pieces, but small juveniles will need them cut into thin slices. Use a vegetable peeler to make especially thin slices for hatchlings. Adding a larger piece of a vegetable to the water will keep your turtle entertained while trying to wear it down, but some smaller turtles might get discouraged with an overly large piece that they can't easily bite into.

There is a belief among turtle keepers that hatchling sliders won't eat greens. This is just a myth. Even the tiniest slider will usually appreciate a bit of romaine lettuce or a piece of anacharis.

Outdoor Bounty

Many yard and garden plants make good slider food. The leaves from mulberry trees (*Morus* species); weeds such as common plantain (*Plantago major*), dandelion (*Taraxacum officinale*), lamb's quarters (*Chenopodium album* and *C. berlandieri*), chickweed (*Stellaria media*), henbit (*Lamium amplexicaule*), and white clover (*Trifolium repens*) can be used in season. Make sure that the dandelion is a true dandelion and not a variety of the milk-thistle plant. As with any edible weed or wild plant, don't offer it unless you are positive of its identification. There

are edible weed field guides available online or at libraries and book stores. You can also consult with a county or university agriculture extension.

Make sure no pesticides or other chemicals are used on the yard or garden and that plants are not harvested from roadsides where chemicals from cars and road work might contaminate the plants. Wild plants often have very high amounts of beneficial nutrients, but they can also have very high amounts of oxalic acid and nitrates, so feed in relatively small amounts.

Aquatic Plants

Sliders dine on many different aquatic plants in the wild, so it's natural to try to include some in a pet slider's diet. Some species you can feed your slider are anacharis (*Elodea* species), frogbit (*Limnobium* species), duckweed (*Lemna* species), water hyacinth (*Eichhornia crassipes*), water lettuce (*Pistia stratiotes*), salvinia (*Salvinia natans*), and water fern (*Azolla caroliniana*). If offering a plant with substantial roots or underwater stems, such as water lettuce or anacharis, rinse the plant well and carefully pick it over to remove snails, which may carry internal parasites, specifically flukes. Aquatic plants can be found in outdoor ponds or purchased from some pet stores and plant nurseries.

Fruits

Apples, nectarines, pears, mangos, cantaloupe and other melons, strawberries, blueberries, other berries,

FAMILY-FRIENDLY TIP

A Weed Walk

One way to add variety to a turtle's diet and get fresh air is to take the family for a nature hike or weed walk. A walk around the yard or a local hiking trail can yield all sorts of edible weeds and insects, earthworms, or other invertebrates for the turtle's diet. Take along a weed or plant guide and insect field guide to identify plants and animals found along the way. Remember to bring containers for the bugs. Checking under rocks and pieces of wood can yield free earthworms and pillbugs—and is an activity most kids love!

papayas, and figs all make great treats for aquatic turtles. Rinse all fruits well, and peel apples and other hard-skinned fruits. Turtles seem to especially like blueberries, which are nutrient-dense.

Animal Protein

Although wild sliders tend to eat less animal protein as they get older, they still relish it no matter their age. However, protein should make up no more than 40 percent of the total diet. Some commercial diets contain up to 40 percent protein, so keep this in mind when adding animal protein to the diet.

You can add more greens and fewer pellets on some days to help balance out a treat of feeder fish or cooked chicken. Daily values are less important than having a balanced diet from week to week, so don't get overly concerned on percentages; as long as the diet is balanced over time, your slider should be fine.

Meat

Plain *cooked* meats such as fish, shrimp, and chicken are fine slider foods. A simple treat can be prepared by boiling a raw or frozen shrimp or piece of chicken in a cup of water in the microwave or on the stove. You could also bake it. Do not use additional oil or seasoning on food prepared for a turtle. A bit of boiled chicken liver or beef liver is a very good source of vitamin A, but don't offer too much in one sitting. You can offer peeled boiled eggs as an infrequent treat.

Live Fish

Turtles will eat live feeder fish, such as guppies and mosquito fish. Try to avoid goldfish and rosy reds, as they contain thiaminase, an enzyme that destroys vitamin B_1, but one every month or so won't hurt your turtle. Be aware that a turtle may not eat all live fish he is fed, and you may end up with extra pets over time.

Insects and Other Invertebrates

Commercially raised feeder insects sold in pet stores or online, such as mealworms, super worms, and silkworms, are acceptable additions to the diet;

again, moderation is the key. Some keepers have reported gut impaction in turtles fed large amounts of mealworms. You can offer your turtle field insects and other invertebrates such as June bugs, grasshoppers, and woodlice (also known as pillbugs or roly-polies), but only if you take them from areas that are known to be free of pesticides. Crickets are known to be sources of nematode parasite contamination, even store-bought crickets, so try to avoid crickets. If you raise feeder roaches for other animals, they are also fine for turtles.

Avoid feeding snails, because they can be carriers of parasitic flukes. If you propagate snails in a separate container without any other animals (fish and other animals are intermediate vectors of the parasite), they will be safe to offer as food. Avoid wild-caught caterpillars, as some feed entirely on toxic plants (such as tomato leaves or milkweed) that can pass harmful chemicals onto your pet.

Do not use earthworms used in manure piles, as these worms may contain high amounts of bacteria and parasites. You can collect earthworms from your yard or local woods as long as chemicals aren't used in the surrounding area. They can also be ordered online or purchased as bait from convenience stores or sporting good stores.

Mice

If you have pinkie mice on hand for other animals, it's okay to offer a pre-killed pinkie to a turtle. It's a good idea to use pre-killed frozen pinkies (frozen for at least 72 hours), as freezing will kill any parasites that they might be carrying. Allow the mouse to thaw to room temperature all the way through before offering it to your slider.

Cuttlebone

Bird keepers are most familiar with cuttlebone. It's actually the bony internal shell of a cuttlefish, which is similar to a squid. The thick, softer part of the cuttlebone can be nibbled or chewed upon by turtles, tortoises, and birds to provide extra calcium. Since many captive reptile diets seem to be lacking in calcium or have a poor calcium-to-phosphorus ratio, it's a good idea to offer cuttlebone. You can float large

This young slider is about to eat an aquatic turtle pellet. Pellets are a good staple diet for aquatic turtles.

pieces in the water for the slider to nibble on as he sees fit. Make sure to remove the thin, hard back portion of the cuttlebone before offering it to a turtle; the hard backing can be sharp and should never be offered to turtles. It might be helpful to soak it in a bowl of water over night before using a butter knife to remove the hard backing. Cuttlebone is most often found in the bird section of pet stores, but some distributors now package it for reptiles. Although most modern commercial diets now contain adequate amounts of calcium, it's still a very good idea to let your turtle have free access to cuttlebone.

The Expert Knows

Foods to Avoid

Raw meats from the grocery store can carry *E. coli* and *Salmonella*, so all meats should be cooked and cooled before being offered. Processed meats, such as lunch meat and hot dogs, contain high amounts of sodium and other chemicals that can be harmful to a turtle, especially if offered long-term. *Never* give fireflies to a turtle or any other animal, as the fireflies contain toxic chemicals. Never offer chocolate or other processed sweets. Avoid avocados and onions. They are known to be harmful to other animals, so it's best to avoid offering them to turtles as well.

Homemade Diet

Some keepers like the idea of making their own turtle food. This enables them to know exactly what goes into their pet's diet. One way to do this is by making a turtle gelatin or "pudding" for turtles. Different recipes exist, but most consist of plain gelatin dissolved in a smaller than normal volume of water and then combined with pureed or grated meats, greens and other vegetables, and vitamin and calcium powder. This mixture is cooled in the refrigerator, then cut into pieces and stored in air-tight containers in the freezer. Individual pieces are thawed and offered to the turtle.

These gelatin diets are highly palatable and can be modified with

carnivorous or herbivorous turtle species in mind. They can be a good way to get a picky eater started on the right foods and then gradually switched to pellets. Plus, if your slider only wants to eat high-protein foods, this is a good way to sneak in greens, vegetables, and vitamins.

Be forewarned that preparing a gelatin diet can be a messy process, and pieces of greens can clog the blades of a food processor, but your turtle will probably love the results. Some people like using ice cube trays for setting the gelatin and for portion control.

Several recipes can be found on the Internet, or you can try the one below. If your turtle takes to it, the amount of animal protein used can be gradually reduced and more vegetables can be added as your slider adjusts to a new diet.

Basic Turtle Gelatin

To make the turtle gelatin you will need the following ingredients:

- 1 box (four 8g packets) of unflavored gelatin

- 1 cup cold water plus ½ cup cold water

- 1 cup diced meat. You can use any combination of the following to equal one tightly packed cup: beef heart or lean beef, chicken breast, shrimp, oyster, fish, and beef or chicken liver. Liver should be no more than 10 to15 percent of the meat. Try to use more than one type of meat. If not using liver in one batch, try to use it in the next batch.

- 1 cup pureed vegetables and fruit. Mix vegetables such as greens, sweet potato, green beans, broccoli, weeds, and other foods listed as acceptable foods. Add a few blueberries or raspberries if possible. Aim for a cup of tightly packed greens and a half cup of diced vegetables. This should equal one cup of pureed vegetables after they are put through a food processor. Try to use a variety between each batch of food.

- ½ teaspoon vitamin supplement

- 1 teaspoon calcium supplement (use phosphorus-free calcium powder; if your slider is indoors, use a calcium powder that contains vitamin D)

Puree the vegetables in a food processor or blender and measure out one cup of puree. Add one cup of vegetable puree to the sauce pan. Discard any excess vegetable puree. Puree the meat and put it in the sauce pan. Rinse the processor or blender with a cup of water and add that water to the pan.

Gently heat the ingredients just to boiling, and then remove from heat.

Dissolve the gelatin in ½ cup cold water and add to the sauce pan. Mix well. Add calcium and vitamin powder and mix well.

Pour into a pie or cake pan and cool in the refrigerator until set, about two or three hours. Cut into pieces and place in an airtight container in the freezer. Store up to a month.

Skipping a Meal

If you're going away for a weekend or a family emergency pops up, your turtle will be fine if he misses a meal or two. You don't have to hire a pet sitter for a long weekend or a short business trip. Timed fish-pellet dispensers that can be used in a slider enclosure are available for when you'll be gone for a few days. Although a healthy turtle in good weight can easily go a week without food, it's best to have someone check on your turtle, filter, and habitat and to offer food if you'll be gone more than three or four days.

Chapter 4

The Healthy
Slider

Many find it surprising that turtles—all reptiles in fact—can suffer from many of the same ailments that people do, and then some. Turtles can contract parasites, develop respiratory infections, skin and shell infections, ear infections, neurological disorders, and even get cancer. Although sliders are very hardy turtles, stress caused by low temperatures, poor water quality, and an improper diet can all lead to illness. Learning how to spot developing illnesses early can save weeks or months of expensive recovery time and keep your turtle happy and healthy.

Weekly Inspections

Each week, inspect your turtle for any changes in appearance. Doing a regular visual exam can help you catch any problems before they develop into larger problems.

Take your turtle out of the water and hold him up. It helps to have a towel handy to dry him off and help hold him. Hold the turtle with a hand on each side of the bridge. If the head is facing you, have your thumbs on the plastron and your other fingers on the carapace. If the nails on the hind feet can reach your hands, you can place one hand under the middle of the plastron and another hand on the middle of the carapace or use a towel or gardening gloves to protect your hands while holding the turtle.

Holding and Turning Your Turtle

To look at the plastron, it is preferable to turn the turtle front to back instead of side to side. Hold the turtle with his head facing you and tilt the body up so that the head is facing the ceiling and the plastron is facing you. When you're done observing the plastron and tail, tilt the plastron back toward the floor so that the turtle's head is again facing you. Although you can turn the turtle from one side to the other side, do not make a complete circle while turning the turtle over; although rare, it is possible to twist the intestines by rotating a turtle in a complete circle from one side, upside down, and then to the other side before being turned right-side-up. If you turn a turtle sideways to look at the plastron, always turn him back the same way you got him there. Avoid quick turns; it's a good idea to take two seconds to turn over a turtle to complete a turn. Don't keep a turtle on his back any longer than necessary, as a turtle feels extremely vulnerable, and thus stressed, while on his back.

Visual Inspection

While holding your slider, pay particular attention to the eyes, mouth, toes, tail, and shell. Press on the shell and check for soft spots or unusual discolorations. Look closely at the marginal scutes to check for loose scutes or discoloration. Check for any unusual swellings or lumps, as well as any cuts or abrasions. Check the mouth and nose for excessive mucus and bubbles, which are signs of a respiratory infection. Look for loose or broken nails. Check the eyes to make sure they're clear and bright, with no puffiness.

Weighing Your Turtle

Weighing your turtle each week is another good idea, as rapid weight loss can be a sign of illness. Smaller turtles can be weighed on gram scales, which can usually weigh a turtle of up to two pounds (0.9 kg). Gram scales are available at most retail outlets and department stores. Larger turtles might need to be weighed on a baby scale or a normal household scale. You can keep track of weekly weight and weekly observations in a notebook or on your computer if you like. That will give you a record of how your turtle has progressed. Since most families have busy lives, a record of observations, vet visits, additions of new tank equipment, food preferences, regular weigh-ins, and any medications given to the turtle can make it easier to track problems if they occur, and it will be helpful to new keepers if you ever have to give away your slider.

Veterinarians

Sliders are very hardy animals, but they can still get sick, even with the best of

FAMILY-FRIENDLY TIP

Let's Do It Together

Children can help with a weekly health check while an adult holds the turtle. Just make sure that fingers and noses don't get too close to the turtle's head, though, as a turtle may try to bite during handling. Explain what to look for, and why it's important to do regular checkups on turtles (and people) to catch small health problems before they turn into bigger problems. An adult and child can compare notes afterward to make sure all areas were checked and to see whether both of the observers saw the same things.

care (although the majority of illnesses they contract are from improper care). Since not all veterinarians are qualified or experienced enough to treat turtles, it's a good idea to find a qualified reptile veterinarian before you need one. You can contact a regional turtle and tortoise club or herpetological society to see whether they can recommend a veterinarian. Online forums are good places to ask as well. You can also contact the Association of Reptilian and Amphibian Veterinarians to search for a veterinarian experienced with turtles. You can find this organization online at www.arav. org or call it at 800-627-0326.

Well-Pet Checkup

It's a good idea to take your turtle to a vet as soon as you get him, to make sure he's healthy. Veterinarians usually call these visits well-pet visits or well-pet checkups. A well-pet check is a good idea as the years go by, just to make sure your pet stays healthy. It is recommended that you take your slider to a well-pet check every two to three years if there are no apparent health issues. Your veterinarian may recommend more or less time between well-pet checks, and you should follow the vet's advice.

It's a good idea to take your new slider to a reptile veterinarian for a checkup soon after you get him and about every other year after that.

Before the Visit

A trip to the veterinary clinic can be confusing, especially for first-time pet owners. When you call to schedule an appointment, ask the receptionist if the veterinarian will need anything in particular from you. Check to see what the prices are for office visits, fecal testing, and blood work so that you'll know what to expect before the appointment. Most veterinarians charge a flat fee each time your pet is brought in for an examination or office visit, and any procedures and testing are charged in addition to the office visit.

During the Visit

Your veterinarian will want to know exactly how you've been housing and caring for your pet, so be prepared to answer questions about enclosure size and type, lighting and heating,

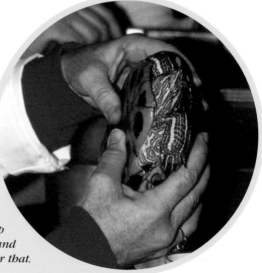

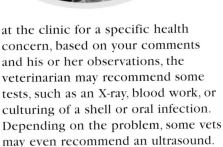

The veterinarian will weigh your turtle as part of the exam. You may also want to buy a scale so you can keep track of your turtle's weight yourself.

water filtration, substrate, tank mates, and feeding your turtle. If you can write down all the specifics before you leave the house (for example, the type or brand name of the UVB light and pelleted foods you're using, how hot your basking spot and water is, or how much and how often you're feeding your slider) this information will help you remember the details when you're at the clinic. A picture is worth a thousand words, so bring a picture of your current enclosure to show the vet if you can. He or she might be able to help you tweak the habitat to improve the health of the turtle.

Once you're at the clinic, a technician or the veterinarian will weigh your turtle. You'll be asked a simple history of the turtle, such as age, how you acquired him, and how long you've had hm. Then the veterinarian will examine the turtle. This should include opening the mouth to look for lesions and general oral health. The vet will palpate the abdomen, tug on the legs to see how fast the turtle reacts (similar to a doctor tapping your knee), and inspect the eyes, tail, and legs to make sure everything is in working order.

If your turtle appears healthy, that may be the end of the exam. If you're

at the clinic for a specific health concern, based on your comments and his or her observations, the veterinarian may recommend some tests, such as an X-ray, blood work, or culturing of a shell or oral infection. Depending on the problem, some vets may even recommend an ultrasound.

If the vet prescribes medications for a sick turtle, make sure you get detailed instructions on how to use them at home, and double check to see that the instructions are printed on the label of all medications. You might want to take notes during the exam to make sure you'll remember everything when you return home. Never be afraid to ask questions of a veterinarian or the staff if you're unsure about a test or course of treatment.

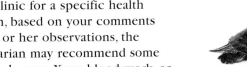

The Healthy Slider

Tests

The vet may perform a variety of tests to determine whether your turtle is healthy, especially if this is the first time you've taken him to the vet. If you're bringing your turtle in for an initial well-pet check, it's not a bad idea to ask for baseline blood work so that the results can be kept on file in case your turtle does become sick. This will enable the vet to compare the results of a healthy slider with the results of a sick animal. Blood work can test liver and kidney function and other important metabolic functions, as well as white and red blood cell counts. The type and amount of white blood cells can indicate what type of infection might be affecting a turtle. If your turtle is listless and/or has a decreased appetite, but no other apparent signs of illness, consider having blood work taken to check for diseases.

It's always a good idea to take a fecal sample so that the veterinarian can check for intestinal parasites.

Even if your turtle is an indoor turtle and a previous fecal sample was clean, it is possible for some foods (such as some live or canned insects) to contain parasites, so a fecal check every few years is a good idea. If you can't get a fecal sample before you leave, most turtles will defecate in the transport carrier during the car ride to the clinic, so it doesn't hurt to feed your turtle a little extra the day or two before a vet visit. The sample should be less than 24 hours old; that's because the eggs of parasites dry out over time, which makes the sample useless. Collect and store the sample in a plastic bag, disposable plastic container, or small disposable jar with a lid and place it in the refrigerator for up to 24 hours before the visit.

A well-pet check is also a good idea to establish ownership of your pet if you don't have proof of when or how you acquired him. If regulations change in the future, or you move to a state that requires a permit to keep your slider, a veterinary record will help show how long you've had your turtle.

Because reptile medicine is still fairly new compared to dog and cat medicine, not every veterinarian is qualified to treat reptiles, especially turtles. For this reason, never let a veterinarian or a technician perform any procedure on your turtle without your permission. If your turtle is going to be weighed and examined in a separate room away from you, make certain that the staff

Deadly Treatment

Ivermectin is commonly used to treat parasites in dogs, cats, and horses. However, it can be deadly to turtles of all kinds. If your veterinarian prescribes ivermectin for your turtle, do not use it! This is a red flag that the vet is not well versed in treating turtles. If you are using ivermectin for another pet, make sure you keep it far away from your turtle.

This is a box turtle with an aural abscess from an ear infection. A slider with this condition will have a similar swelling on his head.

knows they must ask your approval before starting any treatment.

Common Health Problems

Some of the most common ailments of sliders include shell rot, respiratory infections, abscesses, and injuries caused by other turtles. Although good husbandry will prevent most problems from occurring, even the most conscientious of keepers may eventually need to seek veterinary attention for the turtle. This section of this chapter will help you spot some of the health issues that turtles can develop.

Abscesses and Lumps

It is possible for small injuries to go unnoticed, and these injuries could grow into abscesses filled with caseous (a cottage cheese-like) material. Reptiles usually don't form liquid pus the way mammals do, so usually their discharge is in a semisolid form that looks like yellow cottage cheese. You might find such a discharge on the legs, head, tail, or even in the inguinal area between the bridge and hind legs. If you see a swelling that doesn't go away after a few days, consult your veterinarian. Although it is rare, sliders can develop tumors and other cancers and, as with people, early detection is often the key to a successful outcome.

Ear Infections

Turtles have an inner ear similar to humans, and because of this they can develop ear infections. If this happens, you'll notice the ear—also known as the tympanic membrane, the large circular scale on each side of the

Yellow-bellied slider laying eggs. Female turtles sometimes lay eggs even if no male is present, so be prepared to offer yours a nesting area.

head—bulging out. This will require veterinary treatment. Most often the turtle is started on injectable antibiotics and undergoes surgery to open the ear canal and remove hardened pus and debris. The veterinarian usually will send the turtle home with more antibiotics and instructions for flushing the surgical site and packing it with an antibiotic cream for a week or two. The turtle might have to stay dry for some of that time. A common solution for flushing the ear canal after surgery is a mixture of sterile saline with an equal volume of 3 percent hydrogen peroxide, but your veterinarian will provide exact directions for postsurgical care.

Egg Binding

Female turtles, much like female chickens, are capable of laying unfertilized eggs. Some turtles, once they reach sexual maturity, lay once or twice a year for every year of their entire lives, while some lay on random years, and others may never lay eggs. In the wild, red-eared sliders tend to lay eggs between the end of April and the beginning of July. Indoor turtles may lay eggs at any time of the year, so it's best to be prepared so that you can avoid emergencies.

Sliders are capable of laying eggs when they are around 6 inches (15.2 cm) in carapace length. Most turtles prefer to dig a nest to lay their eggs.

If they can't find an appropriate spot, some will just drop the eggs in the water. Others will refuse to lay them and become egg bound. An egg-bound turtle needs immediate veterinary care, as this is a life-threatening condition.

Treatment

In some cases, a dose of the hormone oxytocin administered by a veterinarian will induce egglaying. However, if the eggs have adhered to the lining of the reproductive tract or an egg is too large to pass, surgery may be the only way to save the turtle. Some vets are experienced enough to do this with an endoscope. The vet will pass small tubes through an incision in the inguinal area between the hind leg and the bridge of the shell. However, in some cases, pieces of the female's shell might have to be cut and removed, then epoxied back in place after removing the eggs.

Before inducing egglaying with oxytocin, the turtle will need an X-ray. This will tell you how many eggs are present and may let the vet know whether any are too large or damaged for natural delivery. If the vet decides to use oxytocin, the X-ray will tell you how may eggs the turtle has, so you'll know when all of them pass.

How to Tell Whether Your Turtle Is Carrying Eggs

How can you tell whether your turtle has eggs (technically, this is called being gravid)? Sometimes there's no warning. You may wake up one day to find eggs or egg shards in the aquarium or pond. Many a keeper has been surprised to find eggs in a turtle tank and realize their Donatello is actually a Donna.

To the shock of many, Donna will not only lay eggs at will but also might turn around and eat them! If a slider doesn't have a good laying site, she might lay the eggs out in the open water or on a basking platform. An egg laid in the water isn't identified by the turtle as its own, and she'll consider it an extra protein source. Sometimes the evidence is simply egg shards in the water, but on occasion there may be a smug-looking turtle with egg yolk trailing from her mouth.

If your female is picky about where she lays eggs, she may become nervous and agitated and may attempt to escape the tank. She may also go off her food. One telltale sign is an odd shuffling done with the hind feet while the turtle is at the bottom

More Calcium, Please!

If your turtle has recently laid eggs or you suspect she might be carrying eggs, make sure she has cuttlebone available to chew on. This will help her replace some of the calcium used for egg production.

If your turtle starts spending much more time basking than normal, he could have a respiratory infection.

of the tank. If your female is doing a new sort of funny dance at the bottom of the tank, it might be time to check for eggs.

If you have a light touch, it's possible to palpate the abdomen to check for eggs. You might want a second person to help with this. Hold the turtle with her head pointed toward the ceiling. Grab one hind leg and hold the leg to the side, away from the body. Gently place a finger between the thigh area of the hind leg and the bridge portion of the shell. Tilt the turtle to the side that is being palpated. If there are eggs, you should be able to feel one or two rounded objects, similar to Ping-Pong balls. If you don't notice anything, repeat with the opposite side. Just because you don't feel eggs doesn't mean they aren't there, though. If your

adult female slider is acting lethargic and has a decreased appetite, she might be carrying eggs. If in doubt, set up an egg-laying area, as described in Chapter 2. If your turtle has been acting oddly for more than a week and you suspect she has eggs but hasn't laid them, get her to a veterinarian for an X-ray to rule out egg binding.

If the female has never been with a male, the eggs will be infertile and not hatch. However, if the turtle did mate, the females of some species can store sperm for years after mating. Box turtles have been known to lay viable eggs for up to five years after mating.

General Lethargy and Respiratory Infections

If your turtle is basking all of the time and prefers to stay on his basking platform rather than eat, there is likely a health problem. This is especially true if the turtle is sleeping frequently on his basking platform with his head stretched out. If this action is accompanied by a decrease or lack of appetite, a vet visit is in order. This could be the start of a respiratory infection (or other infection). Turtles are prone to respiratory infections, particularly if kept too cold for long periods of time (apart from a hibernation period).

If the vet cannot find a reason for the lethargy, it's a good idea to ask for blood work to check for elevated white blood cells, indicating an infection of some kind. If the eyes are swollen, the turtle has bubbles coming from the nose or mouth, or he is making a rasping sound with open-mouth breathing, he has a respiratory infection. If caught early, it may be cured by simply raising water temperatures for a few days and adding more vitamin A-rich foods, such as sweet potatoes and collard greens, to the diet. However, serious or prolonged cases usually need antibiotics.

Lopsided Floating

Turtles may develop an inability to float in a normal position. They may float either with one side higher than the other or with the back end higher than the front. If the turtle is floating or swimming with one side higher than the other, this could be a sign of pneumonia. Check your husbandry to make sure temperatures and housing are adequate. An X-ray can confirm whether there's fluid in the lungs; if there is, the turtle may need antibiotics, and the veterinarian may recommend keeping the water warmer than normal.

If just the front or back end is floating higher than the other end, the turtle may simply have intestinal gas, especially if you gave him a new food recently. Review the diet for the last few days and see whether anything new was added. Try feeding just pellets for a few days, and the problem will probably correct itself in a day or two. If it persists, contact your veterinarian.

A turtle that floats and has trouble staying underwater could simply be so underweight that he floats rather than swims. If your new turtle floats all the time rather than swims, it would be a good idea to check with a veterinarian to see whether there is a health problem or whether a special diet is recommended to counter health problems caused by anorexia.

Neck Injuries

In rare cases some aquatic turtles, especially painted turtles, will have a sharp edge on the nuchal scute directly over the neck. This may need to be filed down. Neck injuries are more commonly caused by keeping multiple turtles in close quarters; one turtle is biting the neck of another in a show of dominance. You will need to move the aggressor to a separate enclosure. Once the cause of the injury (usually another turtle) is

removed, the wound will likely heal on its own, although deep wounds may need veterinary care, topical medication, and/or dry-dock time (detailed later in this chapter).

Parasites

Turtles may contract parasites, as other animals do. Internal parasites can damage the lining of the intestines and even lungs (as with flukes) and cause internal tissue damage as they travel through the body. They also weaken the turtle by absorbing nutrients from his system. External parasites remove blood from the host, which can weaken the animal, and may transmit diseases.

Leeches

The only common external parasites for aquatic turtles are leeches, which are the aquatic equivalents of ticks. Leeches are most often found on freshly caught wild turtles, although turtles in backyard ponds may get them. They can be attached to the skin or shell. If you find a leech on your turtle, apply salt to the leech and let the salt sit for a minute, then pull off the leech with tweezers and dispose of it. Make sure that the entire leech is removed and the head isn't still attached to the turtle, as this could lead to an infection. Wipe the area with a disinfectant before putting the turtle back in his enclosure.

Intestinal Parasites

Intestinal parasites are the most common parasites associated with turtles. A fecal float performed at a veterinary clinic can help detect parasites such as hookworms,

Mosquitoes

Mosquitoes may transmit some diseases to turtles (they've been known to transmit the West Nile virus to alligators), but they are usually not a problem for the typical slider keeper. Mosquitoes can breed in any body of water, but they prefer still, shallow water. If you have a pond and are worried about mosquitoes, consider adding a few fish of a small species that can eat mosquito larvae, such as mosquito fish or rosy reds. You can also buy a product called "mosquito dunks" to prevent mosquitoes from breeding in the pond and that is safe for using with turtles.

tapeworms, roundworms, flukes, and protozoans including *Giardia* (often responsible for diarrhea in dogs, cats, and people) and *Coccidia*.

Tapeworms are not uncommon in wild and pet store turtles. Tapeworms will appear as small white segmented pieces in the water; they look almost like pieces of rice. If you see these pieces, try to get them out with a disposable cup or jar, and take them along with your turtle to a veterinarian. The vet will confirm whether they are tapeworms or not. Tapeworms are most often treated with praziquantel. Other common antiparasitic drugs are metronidazole, which is used as an antibacterial and antiprotozoal treatment and also as an appetite stimulant in reptiles,

and fenbendazole, which is used to treat hookworms, roundworms, and pinworms. Whenever possible, let a veterinarian administer these drugs for you, as it is hard for the novice to give these drugs appropriately to an aquatic turtle.

Haemogregarines are a type of blood parasite rarely seen in captive-bred turtles. Although wild turtles can live with the parasite, newly acquired or captured turtles may be so stressed that the inclusion of a blood parasite tips the scales, and the turtle develops anemia as a result. A blood culture is needed to diagnose haemogregarines, and a veterinarian may prescribe antibiotics to treat the parasite. Leeches may be the vector that transmits this parasite.

Prolapse

Reptiles have a cloaca, which is the common opening for the digestive, urinary, and reproductive tract in reptiles. So a turtle lays eggs, defecates, and urinates from the cloaca. In some cases, an organ such as the bladder, oviducts, or penis of a turtle may slip from its normal position and move outside the cloaca. This is known as a prolapse. This is a very serious condition that will need quick veterinary attention to be corrected.

A prolapse may involve the colon, urinary bladder, penis, oviducts and shell glands, and the cloaca itself. In aquatic turtles, it most often involves a female that is having difficulty laying eggs and strains too much. For males,

Prolapse of the penis is a condition occasionally seen in male turtles. It is usually caused by injury from another turtle.

it can involve a penis that might have been damaged by another turtle. Males, especially sub-adult males of about 3.5 to 4.5 inches (9 to 11.4 cm) in carapace length, may "flash" the penis from time to time, especially when handled. This looks like a black or purplish black bulge hanging from the cloaca. If a turtle flashes, the penis usually withdraws after a few seconds to a minute. If this happens in the water, another turtle might bite it, resulting in an injury that prevents the turtle from retracting the penis. In other cases, intestinal parasites might cause so much irritation that part of the cloaca or colon prolapses from straining. Polyps and tumors can also cause this problem. Prolapses may occur in turtles with poor muscle tone, such as those that aren't getting enough calcium or vitamin D.

If your slider has a prolapse, keep the area moist or keep the turtle in his enclosure until you get to a veterinarian. If there are other turtles in the enclosure, you'll have to move the turtle to a separate container until you can seek treatment for the turtle. You might have to remove the turtle from a filter source, as suction from an intake hose might make the problem worse. Transport the turtle on damp newspaper in a plastic container, or use plastic wrap to loosely diaper the tail area and tape the edges of the plastic to the top and bottom shell.

A prolapse usually requires surgery of some sort. In severe cases, the affected tissue may need to be removed. Corrective surgery may involve suturing the colon to the interior body wall to hold it in place.

Shell and Skin Problems

All sliders are supposed to have 13 inner scutes on the carapace. There are five vertebral scutes going down the middle of the shell, and four pleural or costal scutes on each side of the vertebral scutes. Occasionally you might see a slider that has more than 13 scutes, or less often, a slider with less than 13 scutes. This is thought to be the result of improper egg incubation conditions, but it has no impact on the health of the turtle. A slider with extra scutes shouldn't have any health issues; it just makes him easier to pick out of a crowd!

A healthy slider in properly filtered water and a good basking spot never needs any creams applied to the shell—he will need very little, if any, shell maintenance. Although stores may carry shell conditioners, they are completely unnecessary. Fungal and bacterial infections can even be made worse by these products. If you think there is a problem with the shell or skin, it's best to check with a veterinarian rather than buying something off the shelf.

Shedding Scutes

Don't be surprised if you occasionally find thin layers of scutes at the bottom of the tank or stuck to the intake of a filter. This is normal. Sliders will naturally shed the top layer of each scute on the shell. How often this happens depends on the age of the turtle and how fast he's growing. If the diet is amiss, the basking area is subpar, or other health issues are present, sometimes the scutes won't shed properly, and there will be a build-up of unshed scutes. In severe cases, the turtle's shell looks like a pine cone! Time and corrected husbandry usually resolve this situation.

Occasionally a loose scute can trap water and debris between the old and new keratin. This allows algae and bacteria to build up, which can lead to shell rot. If you notice fluid under

Sliders shed scutes from their shells as they grow. These are the shed scutes from a yellow-bellied slider.

a scute, try to gently lift up the edge of the scute. If it can come up easily, it's probably safe to remove the scute. If it doesn't lift easily, leave it be but monitor it closely to see that it does eventually come off.

You can also use 3 percent hydrogen peroxide, found in any pharmacy and most grocery stores in the health section, to try to lift off a partially shed scute. Making sure to keep the hydrogen peroxide out of the turtle's eyes, nose, and mouth, pour some of it on the shell and let it sit for five minutes. If there is dirt, algae, or trapped bacteria at the edge of a loose scute, the hydrogen peroxide will bubble and help remove some of it. Afterward, rinse well and scrub the shell with a soft toothbrush to remove any flaking keratin or debris. Letting the turtle sit in dry dock for an hour or so will help the shell dry so that you can see where loose scutes are peeling up.

Some keepers swear by wheat germ koi pellets if their turtle is having a hard time shedding scutes. These are sold at some plant nurseries, specialty pet stores, and online catalogs as a cool-weather food for pond fish. They contain high levels of vitamin E. Alternate the koi pellets with the usual pelleted foods for a few weeks to see whether it helps with shedding. Do not use wheat germ pellets as the sole food source.

Although wild turtles often have a lot of algae on their shells, it is best to gently scrub it off your pet turtle regularly.

Algae

Although wild turtles often have algae on their shells, it's a good idea to periodically scrub your turtle's shell if algae builds up. Algae may pit the shell and may mask an unshed scute, an early infection, or other injury on the shell. Children can help scrub the shell with a soft toothbrush and room-temperature water.

Skin Shedding

Turtles will shed pieces of skin periodically. Under times of stress, more skin may shed. If it seems that your turtle is constantly shedding skin or there are raw patches of skin, it would be a good idea to check with a veterinarian to see whether there is a deficiency or overdose of vitamin A or an infection. Check the enclosure to make sure there are no sharp edges in the enclosure that the turtle could be rubbing against.

Shell Rot

Shell rot is a generic term for any infection of the shell. A more accurate term is ulcerative shell disease. Any of a variety of organisms can cause shell rot, including bacteria and fungi. In some cases more than one pathogen may be responsible, such as two types of bacteria or a combination of bacteria and yeast. Typically an infection starts when there is a scratch on the shell or a partially unshed scute traps bacteria underneath. Turtles kept in crowded conditions may scratch or bite each other, or a rough basking spot may abrade the shell, leaving an opening for pathogens. Sliders kept without proper heat or a basking spot may be unable to properly shed their scutes and may have depressed immune systems.

If the infection goes undetected long enough, it can spread from the superficial layers of keratin to the bone underneath, and even into the body cavity and blood supply. This

The Expert Knows

Failure to Thrive

Occasionally hatchlings will have failure-to-thrive syndrome. These babies may eat and behave normally at first, but they gradually decrease in energy and eventually develop a soft shell despite the best food, lighting, and care. They tend to stay small and usually don't live more than a year. Although any hatchling turtle may be fragile, these failure-to-thrive hatchlings are usually the result of inappropriate housing before sale, severe dehydration during shipping, or improper conditions during artificial refrigerator hibernation. Since the bulk of slider eggs hatch in the late summer and fall, slider hatchlings purchased between January and June are at a high risk of failure-to-thrive syndrome, as they may have been stored in artificial refrigerator hibernation until sold to a distributor.

89

is called septocemia, or in laymen's terms, blood poisoning. It will eventually kill the turtle.

The sooner shell rot is discovered, the less time it will take to cure and heal, and the less aggressive the treatment required. Although shell rot is more often found in turtles without proper water filtration, it can happen to any turtle. If shell rot is discovered,

it's important to review housing and husbandry to determine how the problem started and how to prevent it from recurring.

Superficial shell rot may be treated with a thorough cleansing and removal of harmful matter from the affected area and the application of a disinfectant, such as povidone iodine solution, or a dilute chlorohexidine

Two hatchlings showing two different forms of shell rot (circled in red). There are many causes, but shell rot is most common in crowded and filthy conditions.

Tube Feeding

Sliders that are extremely ill and not able to eat for extended periods of time, such as those that have suffered head injuries or been hit by a car, might need a pharyngostomy tube. A pharyngostomy tube is a thin, hollow, flexible plastic tube inserted by an experienced veterinarian through a small incision in the neck into the esophagus and stomach while the turtle is under anesthesia. It's held in place by stitches on the outside of the neck, and the long exterior end is taped to the carapace to hold it in place. Oral medication and food in the form of a liquid slurry is added via a syringe at the exterior opening of the tube.

Although this procedure may seem extreme, it's actually much easier and less stressful than trying to force-feed a turtle. Most turtles don't seem to realize it's even there. When the turtle is well enough to eat on his own, he can eat if he wants to even if the tube is still in place. Once the turtle is eating on his own, the tube is removed during an out-patient office visit at the veterinary clinic. Obviously, a pharyngostomy tube is used only in dire circumstances, and only by a qualified veterinarian.

solution. If you are allergic to shellfish or iodine, do not use a povidone iodine solution. Use a soft toothbrush lightly to scrub the area with 3 percent hydrogen peroxide. Rinse the shell and apply the disinfectant to the area, then let the turtle sit in dry dock for an hour before rinsing off the disinfectant. Blot the area dry and apply a triple antibiotic ointment before placing the turtle back into the water.

More serious cases may require surgical debridement under general anesthesia at a veterinary clinic, followed by injectable antibiotics. The turtle may need to stay days or weeks in dry dock. When in doubt, consult a qualified veterinarian. If surgical debridement is required, silver sulfadiazine, an antimicrobial cream used for human burn victims, may

be applied to the affected area daily until healthy connective tissue begins to form. Cover the area completely in a thin layer of this ointment. A veterinarian must prescribe silver sulfadiazine and antibiotics.

Shell rot most often appears as a lighter area of shell that seems out of place from the normal coloration. If pressed, it might be softer than the rest of the shell and have a foul-smelling caseous material under the keratin. Bacterial shell rot smells completely different from the normal aquatic smell of a water turtle, so don't be afraid to get your nose close to the shell when inspecting a turtle. In severe cases, the keratin will lift easily and may come away with pieces of thick caseous material and even infected bone. In rare cases, an

Red-eared slider with a severely deformed shell, most likely from being kept too dry and being fed an inadequate diet.

infection might start below the keratin and travel directly to the bone, leaving a shell with a perfect appearance but a foul smell and a soft area of shell.

As the shell heals, the area may harden and turn pale and look similar to bone before it is shed and healthy new shell is revealed. In many cases, new shell will be darker and rougher than the original shell. This is especially common with turtles that have received burns to the shell.

Soft Shell

Turtles lacking enough calcium, vitamin D_3, and/or UVB light can develop soft shells and bone deformities. This is often called metabolic bone disease (MBD). Too much phosphorus in the diet can inhibit the absorption of calcium as well, but this is usually not the case with aquatic turtles. Too much vitamin A can also inhibit absorption of vitamin D_3, but this usually isn't a problem for aquatic turtles that get a healthful diet

Shell Injuries

Occasionally accidents may happen, such as a turtle escaping an enclosure and falling on a hard floor, resulting in a cracked shell. Until you can get him to a veterinarian, you can rinse the shell with sterile saline to clear

Emergency Care

It's a good idea to keep a first aid kit on hand for emergencies. Outdoor turtles may encounter a predator or a neighbor's dog may jump the fence to find a turtle in a pond. You may happen upon a wild turtle that has been hit by a car, or your turtle may fall accidentally from an unsecure tank top and crack his shell.

A kit may include:

- Sterile saline for flushing and cleaning wounds
- Povidone iodine for disinfecting wounds and treating fungal and bacterial infections
- Sterile gauze and surgical tape for covering wounds
- Triple antibiotic ointment to cover small wounds or cracks.
- Styptic powder to stop bleeding from a broken claw or superficial cracked shell.
- 3 percent hydrogen peroxide for cleaning and for use during and after removal of dirt from a shell
- Tweezers
- Magnifying glass
- Cotton swabs for applying disinfectant and triple antibiotic ointment
- A clean towel or two
- Your veterinarian's phone number (plus the phone number of an emergency clinic if your vet does not have 24/7 service; make sure the emergency clinic treats reptiles)

out dirt, and then apply povidone iodine with sterile gauze. The turtle may need to spend the night in dry dock before being returned to his enclosure, to ensure that bleeding has stopped before he goes back into the water. Deeper or extensive breaks may need a partial patch to the area or antibiotics—your veterinarian can determine the best course of treatment.

Swollen or Irritated Eyes
Turtles with respiratory infections often have swollen eyes. In severe cases, pus forms under the sealed eyelids. Although swollen eyes are occasionally the result of hypovitaminosis A (lack of vitamin A in the diet), more often than not it's a secondary result of a respiratory infection. The problem usually corrects itself once the turtle is on antibiotics, although sterile saline may be used to rinse the eyes for a few days.

The eyes themselves can become infected, especially if the water quality is poor. Rarely the tear ducts can become inflamed and infected. In these cases, a veterinarian may prescribe eye drops and/or injectable antibiotics, as well as a change in husbandry.

As bad as it sounds, turtles have been known to bite each other on the eyes, so if you keep more than one turtle, this is a possibility. Keep an eye on how two or more turtles interact with each other.

Toenail and Foot Problems
Healthy sliders will never need their nails trimmed. Adult males of slider, painted, redbelly, cooter, and some map turtle species have longer front claws than the females do. The front claws on the males of these species are supposed to be long—do not cut them! Very rarely, if a slider has been kept in poor conditions, such as out of the water too often, the claws might be overgrown. If in doubt, consult with a veterinarian or the local turtle and tortoise society to see whether the claws need to be trimmed. Be aware that inexperienced

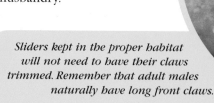

Sliders kept in the proper habitat will not need to have their claws trimmed. Remember that adult males naturally have long front claws.

Dry puffy eyes are the most common sign of a vitamin A deficiency in turtles. Feeding your slider a proper diet will prevent this problem.

veterinary technicians may try to trim the claws of male sliders

Occasionally a slider might catch a claw on a basking platform or aquarium decoration, causing an injury or infection. Rarely a broken or injured claw can lead to a bone infection in the foot. If an injury doesn't appear to be healing after a few days, check with your veterinarian to see whether antibiotics are needed. A very swollen foot or leg is cause for a trip to the veterinary clinic, as it could indicate a broken bone or serious infection.

Turtles have been known to nip off the toes and tail tips of other turtles, so be aware of this possibility.

Vitamin A Deficiency and Toxicity

Too little vitamin A is called hypovitaminosis A, and too much is called hypervitaminosis A or sometimes vitamin toxicity. True vitamin A deficiency in turtles is rare these days, thanks to improved commercial diets and better information. However, an unbalanced diet can lead to hypovitaminosis A. Giving your turtle too much vitamin supplement is the usual cause of hypervitaminosis A.

The most common symptoms of vitamin A deficiency are puffy, dry eyes and excessive skin shedding,

Helping a Wild Turtle

You may find injured wild sliders or other turtles on the side of the road. These turtles usually have serious injuries that need to be treated by a veterinarian or licensed wildlife rehabilitator. Most state wildlife agencies keep a list of wildlife rehabbers in their state, so you should be able to locate one through your state office.

There are some things you can do to help the injured turtle until you can get him to a more experienced caregiver. If there are extensive deep breaks in the shell or large holes that expose underlying tissue, cover them with sterile gauze and tape it to the shell. This will help keep flies and other insects from the injured area. If the shell is broken in several pieces so as to prevent gauze from being taped in place, put a towel over the turtle to cover it. Keep the turtle in a cardboard box or plastic tote with a towel or shredded newspaper in a dark, quiet place at room temperature until the turtle can be taken to a vet or rehabber. An injured turtle may not be able to thermoregulate properly and could overheat if placed under a heat lamp.

If you do take in an injured wild turtle, do not offer him food until he has received veterinary attention, and do not offer water unless directed to by a veterinarian or rehabber. A severely injured turtle may not be able to process food until blood pressure and other symptoms have been stabilized. If you must offer water, use a heavy bowl that is hard to tip over. Do not include an aquatic section in an injured turtle's enclosure unless a vet says to do so. It's best to keep wounded turtles dry. Make note of the exact location you found the turtle so that he can be released where he was found (or near there if there's no water where you found him) once he has recovered at the rehabber's facility.

but lethargy, decreased appetite, and a compromised immune system may also occur. The turtle becomes prone to various infections, especially respiratory infections. A vitamin A deficiency can usually be corrected with a proper diet.

The signs of an overdose are similar to the signs of a deficiency but can be more severe: sloughing skin and puffy eyes. An overdose can be extremely painful, as the skin may slough off to leave bloody raw patches, and may lead to death from infection and toxicity. An overdose is rare but may be caused by giving injections of vitamin A, giving the turtle large amounts of vitamin supplements, or regularly feeding him large amounts of liver. Symptoms of a dietary overdose will decrease if the levels of vitamin A in the diet are reduced to appropriate levels. However, prognosis of an overdose from an injection of vitamin A is often poor.

Vitamin A—along with vitamins D, E, and K—is a fat-soluble vitamin, which means that there needs to be some fat in the diet for the vitamins to be properly absorbed. Most pelleted foods have some fat in the formula, and insects and meat will have fat. There are two kinds of vitamin A, retinol and various carotenoids. Carotenoids include beta-carotene, which is the most active and safest way to take vitamin A to avoid vitamin A toxicity. In general, green leafy vegetables are good sources of carotenoids, although carrots, sweet potato, broccoli, and pumpkin are also good sources. It is impossible to overdose on carotenoids, although large amounts may interfere with the absorption or metabolism of other vitamins, such as vitamin D.

Vitamin A supplements are more likely to contain retinol, which is toxic in large amounts. So if a veterinarian recommends an injection of vitamin A for a sick turtle, ask that half of the recommended dosage be given, as it is easy to overdose with injectable vitamin A. Natural sources of retinol include liver and egg yolk; although these foods may be offered in small amounts, don't make them a large part of the daily diet.

Administering Medications

If your turtle needs oral medications, it's usually best to leave it to the veterinarian to administer with a ball-tipped cannula. This is a curved metal tube, similar to a long hypodermic needle, with a rounded ball tip instead of a point, that is attached to a syringe. The veterinarian can restrain the turtle's head, gently pry open the mouth, and insert the cannula down the esophagus and directly into the stomach. It sounds rough, but it's fast and efficient if performed by an experienced veterinarian. This is a good way to dose some anti-parasitic medications and antibiotics. Having your veterinarian dose out oral medications this way is preferred, because most keepers aren't comfortable prying their turtles' mouths open, and if too much

For some types of health problems, a turtle needs to be kept dry. A soft towel is a good substrate for a temporary dry enclosure.

medication is placed in the mouth at once it is possible for the turtle to aspirate the liquid into the lungs. On the other end of the spectrum, some of the liquid could fall out of the turtle's mouth. Since medications are often dosed at exact volumes, your turtle wouldn't be getting all of the medication he needs if he doesn't swallow all of it.

Some medications, such as many antibiotics, come in injectable forms. Your veterinarian can show you how to inject the turtle if an injectable antibiotic is prescribed; you then can continue the course of antibiotics at home. Most injections are given in the front legs, and most antibiotics are given intramuscularly (IM). If you're uncertain of how to do this

after watching the veterinarian, or are unwilling to give injections, see whether you can bring the turtle in for a quick visit with a veterinary technician who can give injections in the office. Most antibiotics are given every other day or every third day, depending on the type of antibiotic used. Always follow the directions given by the veterinarian, as many drugs are toxic or ineffective if given incorrectly.

Dry-Dock Time

If a turtle is recovering from an ear abscess, shell injury, or other surgery, he might need to spend time in dry dock. This is a type of hospital enclosure that allows the turtle to stay dry and warm for a period of time. A plastic storage bin or tote makes a good dry-dock tank. A towel or shredded newspaper is used as a substrate so that the turtle can hide if he wants and also to cushion his plastron.

Place a heat lamp on a screen over one end of the enclosure, creating a temperature gradient. The turtle can bask under the light or move to the cooler end as he chooses. You might need to experiment with the wattage of the light to make sure the turtle gets warm enough but doesn't overheat. A regular household 75-watt light bulb is usually a good start. An untippable water bowl can go into the dry dock. If the turtle is constantly tipping the bowl, or is always wetting the injured body part in the water, it might be best to do without a water bowl.

Larger adult turtles can spend the majority of the day in dry dock, but juvenile turtles usually can't go without water that long. A larger turtle might spend the majority of the day in dry dock, going into his regular tank for only half an hour to an hour once or twice a day to drink and eat. Since small turtles can dehydrate faster than larger turtles, juveniles might need to be treated in the reverse order, spending a few hours or overnight in dry dock and staying in their regular enclosure the rest of the time. Consult with your veterinarian for advice on how best to dry-dock your turtle.

Because turtles in dry dock are often on antibiotics that can be rough on the kidneys, it's important that sliders being treated stay properly hydrated. Make sure your turtle gets to drink and soak at least once a day unless fluids are being added through a pharyngostomy tube.

Making a Hard Decision

At some point, any animal may become ill and require extensive testing or veterinary treatment. Not everyone is prepared for this type of expense. If you cannot afford treatment, discuss the options with your veterinarian. Some veterinarians offer a payment plan to customers. If you absolutely cannot afford treatment, and your slider is suffering, do not be afraid to discuss euthanasia. A good veterinarian can euthanize or "put to sleep" a turtle in a painless, humane way. Some people cannot bring themselves to consider this option, but euthanasia is preferable to allowing an animal to suffer with an untreated painful illness. Most veterinarians provide a service for disposing of a euthanized animal, or you may wish to take your pet with you for burial. If you don't have access to a veterinarian who treats turtles but you must have your pet euthanized, ask your veterinarian to consult with a reptile veterinarian found through the Association of Reptilian and Amphibian Veterinarians.

Chapter 5

Similar Species

If you've decided that a slider isn't for you, or you want to expand your turtle keeping repertoire, some of the following turtles might be of interest to you. Some of these stay smaller than sliders, which makes them more desirable for novice keepers.

Mississippi map turtles are one of the most available species of map turtles. Like other maps, they thrive only when the water quality is excellent.

Map Turtles

The map turtles (*Graptemys* species) are beautiful turtles that can be challenging to keep as pets. They are called map turtles because the intricate lines on their shells resemble the markings on contour maps. Common varieties of pet map turtles are the common, false, Mississippi, and Ouachita maps (*Graptemys geographica, G. pseudogeographica, G. kohnii,* and *G. ouachitensis ouachitensis* respectively). It's important to know the species of map turtle you have, as some

stay much smaller than others (7 inches to 13 inches [17.8 to 33 cm] at full adult size). Males are about half the size of the females, although this varies by species. Males of some species have longer front claws than females, while the males of other species do not.

Wild map turtles eat a similar diet to sliders, except that males tend to eat primarily insects and females eat a large amount of gastropods and mollusks. They may eat snails, insects, crayfish, fish, and aquatic vegetation. However, the bulk of their

Map turtles, such as this Ouachita map, are some of the prettiest pet turtles. However, they are not the best choice for first-time turtle keepers.

The striped mud turtle is the most colorful of the United States species.

diet is gastropods. Juveniles tend to eat more insects.

Care is basically the same for map species as for sliders. Keep in mind that map turtles tend to be shyer turtles than sliders and are far less forgiving of husbandry errors than sliders. Map turtles need extremely clean filtered water, as these are turtles primarily of fast-flowing rivers. Frequent water changes are important for the health of map turtles. They also tend to need slightly warmer basking temperatures than sliders. They have thinner shells than sliders, so shell rot can be especially problematic for map turtles.

These turtles also have crushing plates in their mouths that can become overgrown if fed a typical captive diet. In the wild, they feed on harder foods such as crustaceans and mollusks. Without hard foods, the crushing plate can become so overgrown that the turtle has trouble closing its mouth. Such a problem can be corrected by a trip to the veterinarian, who can grind down the crushing plates while the turtle is under general anesthesia. Keeping crushed coral in the tank for the turtle to chew on can help keep the crushing plate in good health. You can also propagate aquatic snails to feed your map turtle.

Mud Turtles

Mud turtles (*Kinosternon* species) are very similar to musk turtles in appearance, temperament, and

sliders. The southern species may require slightly warmer water temperatures than sliders, so be sure to check the husbandry requirements of each species individually. The striped (*K. baurii*) and eastern (*K. subrubrum subrubrum*) muds are often available to hobbyists. Most adult musk and mud turtles in the pet trade will be wild-caught, but breeders often have captive-bred juveniles for sale. Be aware that the Mexican and Central American species can grow larger than the United States species.

husbandry. These turtles are found from the northern United States south to Peru. The mud turtles of the United States rarely grow beyond 4 inches (10.2 cm) in carapace length. They also have a double hinged plastron and can close the shell completely when frightened.

Although they may tend to be more nocturnal than sliders, painteds, and maps, the mud turtles are small, hardy, and have interactive personalities once they've settled into a permanent home. Much like musk turtles, muds tend to be more carnivorous than

The razorback musk turtle is the largest species in the United States. It ranges from Alabama to eastern Texas and Oklahoma.

Musk Turtles

Although the musk turtles (*Sternotherus* species) of the United States aren't as flashy as sliders, painteds, or maps, they have a quiet charm of their own; they also stay quite small. The largest species reaches a maximum length of 6 inches (15.2 cm). In the wild they are found from New England, Quebec, and southern Ontario to Florida and west to Wisconsin and central Texas. They have a gray-brown to black carapace that's rather plain in adults. Juveniles have spots or dark radiating streaks on the carapace. Musk turtles get their name for the distinctive (and fairly unpleasant) odor they release when they feel threatened.

The common musk turtle (*S. odoratus*), or stinkpot, is the most common species both in nature and in the pet trade. The razorback musk (*S. carinatus*) is the largest United States species and also the prettiest. Male and female musk turtles are generally the same size, but males have a noticeably larger tail and a slightly concave plastron.

In the wild musk prefer waterways with slow-moving currents and soft bottoms, but you can find them in lakes and ponds, too. They prefer shallow water, which makes a long or breeder tank preferable over a regular or tall tank. If you are keeping a musk turtle with deeper water, he will need

Painted Turtles

Painted turtles (*Chrysemys picta* subspecies) are hobbyist favorites. They start off less flashy than sliders, but unlike sliders they retain their bright colors into adulthood. The skin is black to olive with red and yellow stripes running down the neck, legs, and tail. The shell is olive to black with yellow or red borders on the marginal scutes. Painteds are relatively hardy and don't grow as large as sliders. The care for painted turtles is the same as that of sliders.

There are four subspecies of painted turtles; all are native to North

a way to climb to the surface, such as a ramp, trellis, piled stones, or a piece of drift wood long enough to reach from the floor of the tank to the surface of the water. They've been known to climb up to 6.5 feet (2 m) on small tree trunks over the water. When startled, they will drop back into the water—and occasionally into the lap of surprised boaters!

The captive feeding habits of musks are similar to sliders, and they will sample just about anything. They tend to be more carnivorous and eat plant matter only occasionally. Hatchlings are tiny and may be very fragile.

The western subspecies of the painted turtle is the largest, reaching lengths up to 10 inches (25.4 cm).

Southern painted turtles are common in the pet trade and are found naturally from extreme southern Illinois to the Gulf Coast of Louisiana.

America. Southern painteds (*C. picta dorsalis*) have a broad red stripe down the middle of the carapace, but the other subspecies may have a thinner stripe as well. As with sliders, the males have longer front claws than females. Males are smaller than females. Female western painteds (*C. picta bellii*) may get up to 10 inches (25.4 cm) long, but the other subspecies stay smaller. Male eastern and midland painteds (*C. picta picta* and *C. picta marginata* respectively) usually reach about 4 to 5 inches (10.2 to 12.7 cm) in carapace length. Southern painteds stay even smaller, making them a preferred aquarium turtle. There are several captive breeders of painted turtles, although a western painted in a pet store is more likely to be wild-caught.

Be aware that male painteds can be very aggressive with females of any species. It's best not to mix male painteds with females, unless the enclosure is especially large with lots of hide spots and visual barriers.

Resources

General Care

Discover Life
(turtle identification flowchart)
www.discoverlife.org/
mp/20q?guide=Turtles

Melissa Kaplan's Herp Care Collection
www.anapsid.org

RedEarSlider.com
www.redearslider.com/

Tortoise Trust
www.tortoisetrust.org/

Turtle Forum
www.turtleforum.com/

The Turtle Puddle
www.turtlepuddle.org/

World Chelonian Trust
www.chelonia.org/

Pond And Aquarium Resources

FishLore.com
(aquarium volume calculator)
www.fishlore.com/
ConversionCalculator.htm

Pelomedusa.com
pelomedusa.com/Tanks.html

Robyn's Pond Page
www.fishpondinfo.com/pond.htm

Turtle Ponding
web.me.com/drrich2/Turtle_Ponding/
Chapters_1_-_3.html

The Water Garden
watergarden.com/calculate/liner_
results.php

Turtle and Tortoise Societies, Herpetological Societies, and Rescues

California Turtle & Tortoise Club (CTTC)
www.tortoise.org/

Center for Biological Diversity
www.biologicaldiversity.org/

Chicago Herpetological Society
www.chicagoherp.org/

Colorado Reptile Humane Society
Telephone: 303-776-2070
Fax: 303-776-5206
E-mail: info@corhs.org
www.corhs.org/

Gulf Coast Turtle and Tortoise Society
1227 Whitestone Lane
Houston, Texas 77073
Telephone: 866-99-GCTTS (42887)
www.gctts.org/

Mid-Atlantic Turtle and Tortoise Society (MATTS)
P.O. Box 22321
Baltimore, MD 21203
www.matts-turtles.org

New York Turtle and Tortoise Society (NYTTS)
1214 West Boston Post Road
Box 267
Mamaroneck, NY 10543
nytts.org/

Seattle Turtle & Tortoise Club
1728 29th Ave S.
Seattle, WA 98144
E-mail: seattleturtleclub@yahoo.com
seattleturtleandtortoiseclub.com

Turtle Rescue of Long Island
PO Box 359
Centereach, NY 11720
turtlerescues.com/

Veterinary Resources

Association of Reptilian and Amphibian Veterinarians
810 East 10th, PO Box 1897
Lawrence, KS 66044 USA
Telephone: 1-800-627-0326
(Int'l: 1-785-843-1234)
Fax: 1-785-843-6153
www.arav.org

The New York Turtle and Tortoise Society Vet List
nytts.org/nytts/helpnet.htm

Wildlife Rehabilitation Resources

Indiana Turtle Care
P.O. Box 732
New Palestine, IN 46163
www.Indianaturtlecare.com

National Wildlife Rehabilitators Association (NWRA)
2625 Clearwater Rd, Suite 110
St. Cloud, Minnesota 56301
Telephone: 320-230-9920
Fax: 320-230-9920
E-mail: nwra@nwrawildlife.org
www.nwrawildlife.org/

Wildlife Rehabber
www.wildliferehabber.com/

Books

Cook, Tess. *Box Turtles*. TFH Publications, Inc.

Hellweg, Michael R. *Raising Live Foods*. TFH Publications, Inc.

Highfield, Andrew and Nadine Highfield. *Tortoises: A Beginner's Guide to Tortoise Care*. TFH Publications, Inc.

Kirkpatrick, David T. *Aquatic Turtles*. TFH Publications, Inc.

Pirog, E.J. *Russian Tortoises*. TFH Publications, Inc.

Resources

Index

Boldfaced numbers indicate illustrations.

111

Index

Dedication

This book is dedicated to the members of MATTS and the World Chelonian Trust; the Tortoise Reserve; all the rehabbers, rescuers, and volunteers who have helped me over the years; Dr. Gennaro, who let me work with my first reptiles; and especially my husband who has put up with it all.

About the Author

Karina Smith has a BS in biology from Eastern New Mexico University. She has been the adoptions coordinator for the Mid-Atlantic Turtle and Tortoise Society (MATTS) in Maryland for 11 years. Over 1,000 turtles have been cared for and adopted through MATTS during this time. She works in the biotechnology field helping to create experimental cancer treatments. Katrina shares her home with a western hognose snake, a mud turtle, various foster turtles, a cat, and a husband.

Photo Credits

26kot (via Shutterstock): 43
Altug (via Shutterstock): 93
Aaron Amat (via Shutterstock): 9, 38
Andresr (via Shutterstock): 8 (bottom)
Glenna Babst: 25, 27
Darren Baker (via Shutterstock): back cover (top center)
Joan Balzarini: 76, 77
Colin Barnett: 28
R.D. Bartlett: 40, 95, 102 (bottom)
Murat Baysan (via Shutterstock): 41
Josef Bosak (via Shutterstock): 53
Vince Brach: 104 (top)
Oskar Calero (via Shutterstock): 18
Suzanne L. Collins: 6
Jeff Copeland: 49
Amee Cross (via Shutterstock): 96
Dashingstock (via Shutterstock): 92
Anatoli Dubkov (via Shutterstock) 12
Isabelle Francais: 106, back cover (bottom center)
Paul Freed: 106
William Fuller (via Shutterstock): 74
James E. Gerholdt: 16
Arto Hakola (via Shutterstock): 14
Irina Tischenko (via Shutterstock): 7, 72, back cover (top)

Isantilli (via Shutterstock): 55
J. Kalinowski Photography (via Shutterstock): 35
David T. Kirkpatrick: 105
Yuriy Korchagin (via Shutterstock): front cover
Longshot1972 (via Shutterstock): 51
Marina Mariya (via Shutterstock): 64
Microcosmos (via Shutterstock): 42
Mypokcik (via Shutterstock): 58
Aaron Norman: 36, 102 (top), 103, 107
Mella Panzella: 100
M.P. and C. Piednoir: 21
Sevenke (via Shutterstock): 22
Shutterstock: 60, back cover (bottom)
Smit (via Shutterstock): 17
Katrina Smith: 29, 31, 45, 46, 47, 48, 52, 57, 62, 65, 66, 69, 86, 87, 90
Laurie L. Snidow (via Shutterstock): 4
Karl H. Switak: 8 (top), 11, 13, 80, 94, 104 (bottom)
Dr. Chris Tabaka: 79
Echo Uzzo: 26
Velychko (via Shutterstock): 3, 98
V.R. Valerian (via Shutterstock): 82
Chuck Wagner (via Shutterstock): 88
Feng Yu (via Shutterstock): 33